ENTERING THE 4TH DIMENSIONAL MATRIX

3D Matrix Systems That Will Have to Change

Ronald R. Fellion DD

ENTERING THE 4TH DIMENSIONAL MATRIX

3D Matrix Systems That Will have to Change

Ronald R. Fellion DD

Ronald R. Fellion DD

Copyright 2024 Ronald R. Fellion DD

Published by Ronald R. Fellion DD

All rights reserved. No part of this book may be reproduced by any mechanical, photographic, or electronic process, in the form of a phonographic recording; nor may it be stored in a retrieval system, transmitted, or otherwise be copied for public or private use-other than for "fair use" as a brief quotations embodied in articles and reviews-without prior written permission of the publisher. The intent of the author is only to offer information of a general nature to help you in your quest for emotional and spiritual well-being. In the event you use any of the information in this book for yourself, which is your constitutional right, the author assume no responsibility for your actions or the consequences of those actions to yourself or others.

ISBN:
Paperback ISBN 9798327246928
Hardcover ISBN 9798327247567

Thanks again to my wife, Irina, for giving me the time to write this book.

Ronald R. Fellion DD

Table of Contents

	Introduction..	9
Chapter 1	Religions..	13
Chapter 2	The Medical Field.....................................	28
Chapter 3	Politics...	46
Chapter 4	Financial..	53
	Current Financial Systems.......................	63
	Socialism..	86
	Communism..	90
	Federal Reserve & World Bank..............	112
Chapter 5	AI & Genetic Research............................	120
	Free Energy...	129
Chapter 6	Final Thoughts...	139

Ronald R. Fellion DD

Introduction

Thank you for taking the time to read this book and allowing me to be a part of your spiritual journey. The information I write in my books is based on experiences I've had inside and outside of my body, as well as downloads of information I've received from my higher self. Sometimes this download happens in answer to a question I've asked and at other times in response to what someone else has said or written. Their information acts like a trigger that activates a download within me. The download gives me more information and a deeper understanding of that information.

Our universe and reality are changing and those changes are taking us from what we call the third dimensional matrix into the fourth dimensional matrix.

Several years ago I did a video on some of the changes that will take place in our current matrix programs as we make that shift. Now that some of those changes have started becoming more obvious, I decided it's time to give a more in-depth explanation of those changes and what they are leading us to.

My goal in this book is to give you the bigger picture view of what's happening and why. That way you'll be able to understand how seemingly unrelated changes in different matrix programs are related to an overall goal: the goal of shifting dimensions and humanity moving forward.

I'll focus on the larger matrix programs; religions, the medical field, the economy, and the different types of political systems we currently have, because the changes in these large matrix programs are easier to see and understand. I'll cover some of the changes that have already happened and why they need to change even more.

We'll also look at the affect those changes will have on humanity and our everyday lives.

All the programs of our third-dimensional reality must change because they can't exist or be translated, as the vibrations they are within the fourth dimension. If you've read my other books or watched some of my videos on YouTube, you'll already understand that everything around us is a vibration within a torsion field. The torsion field we are in determines what vibrations we can translate, thus the reality we see and interact with.

For us to get to or shift to the new fifth dimension, we must change or shift our vibration and torsion field. Because the fifth dimension is such a different vibration than the third dimension we're currently in, we have to slowly change the vibrations we can translate and experience from that torsion field. The changes need to be slower because we'll use a physical body in 5D-A rather than the normal light body used in 5D.

Moving into and through the fourth dimension is part of that shifting process.

I'll also cover how AI fits into those changes and why it's a necessary part of our shift to a new universe. The difference in what timeline we follow through the fourth dimension, determines whether AI assists humanity on our spiritual journey forward, or is used to control and destroy humanity.

As with everything I write, I ask you to read it with an open mind and see how the information feels to you as you read it. If it feels right, then see where that information will lead you on your journey and what new vibrations it might open for you. If it doesn't feel right, than it may not be for you at this time, so let it go for now.

If you can't accept that reality and the universe might be more than what science tells you or more than you experience in your everyday life, then this book probable isn't for you.

My goal is as it's always been, not to make you think like me, but to make you think and question what you believe. It's only by questioning what you believe that you can grow beyond or change that belief, to a knowing.

If you have questions or comments, you can leave a comment on any of my YouTube videos. My YouTube channel is Ronald Fellion. If you like what you read or it made you think differently than you did before, please leave a review on Amazon so others can get a better idea if this book is for them.

Ronald R. Fellion DD

CHAPTER 1

RELIGIONS

I've talked a lot about the Matrix program of religion in my other books because religions, or a version of them, are the most widely accepted programs in our reality.

A religious program is much more than a person or group of people believing in a particular God or deity, getting together once a week to worship that being, blindly believing what they're told, singing songs, and making financial offerings.

The Oxford Dictionary defines religion in several ways: the belief in and worship of a superhuman power or powers, especially a God or Gods; ideas about the relationship between science and religion; and a particular system of faith and worship.

The definition I'm talking about when I say it's much more than just doing the church thing, is a pursuit or interest to which someone ascribes supreme importance.

This definition relates to the Matrix programs like politics, sports teams, money, devotion to a country, belonging to a group or club, titles, a brand name, a famous person, and even the daily routine or rituals of many. The term addiction comes to mind.

If you've never thought about the definition or meaning of the term religion and how it relates to your daily life, you should stop reading for a few minutes and do so.

Self-reflection is the only way you'll begin to understand how controlled your daily life actually is.

In this chapter, we'll look at religion related to its first meaning: the belief in and worship of a superhuman power or powers, especially a God or Gods, and how that's changing.

My last book, "Hidden Layers of the Earthly Matrix," explored the major religions relating to how they started and their beliefs in death and the afterlife. This chapter will focus on the current system of religious separation and how that and the other programs of this matrix are changing as we move deeper into the fourth dimension.

The major issue with religions today is their different beliefs relating to their God or Gods and their rituals or practices. It's these differences that are stressed to their members to keep them separated and away from other religions. Highlighting the differences between them helps strengthen the fear they have of those within other groups.

The focus on keeping people from different religions separated from each other is so they can be controlled more easily. This separation will also keep their members from finding the gold hidden within those other religions thereby reducing the chance of them finding the truth and realizing they've been lied to.

As I've stressed in my other books, this third dimension is based on and about creating a world of fear. A population living in constant fear is much easier to control because the fear will keep people from looking inside themselves and growing spiritually. They'll always be looking for that future outside threat and answers or directions from someone else.

Being attacked by the Devil or demons, and constantly worrying that their thoughts will affect their salvation are good examples of religions using that fear program.

As we move into the fourth dimension, this program of separation will be changed. The fourth dimension will involve bringing the programs of separation into one of more unity. A one-world Government and one unified religion are prime examples.

Bringing people together under one umbrella in the fourth dimension is designed to focus their energies into a stronger unified field. That's because the fourth dimension is much larger than the third dimension.

Right now those beings at the top of the fourth dimension are drawing their energy from the lower levels of 4D. The lower levels are drawing their energy from 3D and merging it together forming a more unified stream. Once 3D is absorbed, meaning the 3D universe bubble no longer exists, the current lower level 4D beings wouldn't have that energy coming in. That means the upper level Gods will need to get their energy differently. By creating one world programs, beliefs, rather than programs of separation, they will still be able to unify that 4D stream of energy into what they need.

Like electric wires, a thicker wire will carry more energy farther with less loss.

If you've read my other books where I've talked about how our third dimensional reality was created, or watched my YouTube video, Saturn and the Sun, which explains the same idea, you'll already know about the process of how we moved from the fifth dimension to the third.

I'll give the short version of that story for those of you who are reading my books for the first time.

If you want a more in-depth version you can read my last book or watch the video on YouTube.

Before we came to the third dimension we were fifth dimensional beings consisting of mostly light bodies. Saturn was the Sun of that dimension. When we decided to manifest a third dimension and create what we call a full physical reality and bodies, we knew because of the huge vibrational difference between 5D and 3D, we needed to manifest a fourth dimension to step down our vibrations.

That fourth-dimension and the beings to run it were manifested with the intent to eventually manifest and run a third dimensional pocket universe within the fourth-dimension. It's a pocket universe within 4D which is why the different aliens everyone talks about are from the fourth dimension. It also relates to the firmament mentioned in the Bible. I talk about that in my last book.

Because of the need to step down our vibration slowly, many levels were created within the fourth dimension.

The religious Gods of our 3D reality are the beings in the higher levels of the fourth dimension. They've been there so long, and there are so many levels below them, they believe they were the creators of this world, reality, us, and everything else.

In a way, they are, but they've forgotten how that took place and that we are aspects of them, and they are aspects of us.

We are now moving back into the fourth dimension on our journey back to what will be called 5D-A.

5D-A will be a new universe.

It will be a world in which we'll have all the abilities we had in 5D to manifest with a thought, see how different reality lines play out, manifest the reality any way we want, and so on.

This time, we'll also have a physical body through which we can more completely experience and enjoy that world/s.

As I was writing this part of the book I realized that the heavens promised by religions to their followers if they follow their rules and accept their God, is a watered-down version of my 5D-A reality.

I know the bible as well as other religious books and texts were written to show us how we came here, what our journey here will be like, and where we're going when we leave. Unfortunately for most, some of that information was changed and/or hidden by those from the fourth dimension.

Before you get mad at them, know it's what they were supposed to do to make us seek the truth. They aren't the bad guys as many new agers want us to think. In religions, they're known as Satan, the Devil, and by other names.

Other parts of those writings were rewritten and turned into human-controlled religions. Religions where we are no longer the master of our own journey but one where we must rely on some other being or beings to help us get out of here. Beings we must pledge ourselves and our energy to before that can happen. In case you weren't aware, we wrote all the religious books and papers to leave ourselves clues.

Unfortunately, when we believe other beings have to help us leave this world, we return here to try again. It's the default matrix program because we didn't seek the truth. We took the easy path and just accepted what someone else said was correct.

As I've written before, if you want to leave this limited 3D reality and get to heaven, you need to do the inner work for yourself.

Before you die, let go of the attachments, fears, and regrets your ego hangs onto. That includes your physical body.

Know that when you leave this world, you'll face any fears, regrets, and attachments you're still hanging onto. Know as well, those visions you'll face will be illusions of your mind and not real. Know before you leave this reality what you and your reality are, and that you get to decide where you go and what reality you'll be in.

Do those things and you could end up in 5D-A. What will be your heaven, not one controlled by another being.

Back to how religions are changing as we move deeper into the fourth-dimension.

The fourth dimension is about bringing people back together through technologies and creating one world systems.

Since religion is the most extensive program on the planet, that system will have to change the most. These changes have been going on behind the scenes.

September 14-15, 2022, at the 7th Congress of Leaders of the World and Traditional Religions, Pope Francis, the Grand Imam of Al-Azhar of Islam, and the leader of Judaism got together and all signed a paper bringing the three Abrahamic religions closer together. The paper was called The Document on Human Fraternity and was concerned with how different faiths could live in the same world and areas in peace. The paper was signed in Abu Dhabi, United Arab Emirates.

They declared adopting a culture of dialogue as the path, mutual cooperation as the code of conduct, and reciprocal understanding as the method and standard.

They agreed that all skin colors, genders, races, languages, and cultures are expressions of the wisdom of a religious God's diversity.

They agreed there can be more than one path to God or salvation, and no one should condemn another religion's path.

Since Judaism and Islam don't believe that Jesus is the only path to gaining heaven and salvation, the Catholics have in essence, accepted other paths to heaven outside of the standard biblical Christian path.

Catholics have essentially separated themselves from other Bible believing Christians of this world. In the eyes of some Bible believing Christians, the Catholics have agreed to become one with the anti-Christ.

They base this belief on John 14:6, "I am the way and the truth and the life. No one comes to the Father except through me."

Some Christians have even compared the signing of that document to the building of the Tower of Babel.

On December 20, 2006, the U.N. General Assembly adopted resolution A/61/221 entitled, Promotion of interreligious and intercultural dialogue, understanding and cooperation for peace by all members.

This is all in an effort to bring religions together in the name of peace, even if it means some will have to compromise their founding-fundamental beliefs.

Some Christians see the peace agreement, The Abraham Accords Declarations, that President Trump signed in late 2020 between Israel and several Arab states, including the United Arab Emirates, Bahrain, and Morocco, as another step in compromising religions.

This Agreement stated in part, We, the undersigned, recognize the importance of maintaining and strengthening peace in the Middle East and around the world based on mutual understanding and coexistence, as well as respect for human dignity and freedom, including religious freedom.

This Agreement eventually failed because of a lack of intrinsic valves.

The fact it was signed and at least got them together, even if only for a short time, may have been part of why the agreement was signed by the Pope and others in 2022 at the 7th Congress of Leaders of the World and Traditional Religions.

There are other religious groups that are looking to work closer together and focus more on their areas of shared belief rather than their small differences.

This looking for common ground and working together isn't going to be the singular point or reason that will bring religions together as a one-world religion.

Man's ego is still going to get in the way and the leaders of these different groups aren't going to give up their power and money so quickly. It would've happened long ago if that was all it took to bring religions together.

These papers and cooperation between groups are a way of starting to change the mindset of their followers. It's putting the idea of getting together, unifying, as a possibility into the mind of the religious-the first step, as it were.

What needs to happen in order to bring most all religious groups together under one banner of belief, is a worldwide event. Something that would change the minds of the average religious followers almost overnight.

There will always be holdouts who don't want to give up their beliefs and charismatic leaders of some smaller religious groups will who want to maintain their power and influence. Offering them a position in the new religion would help solve that problem.

I don't know what the event will be that will change the beliefs-Gods of religion. What many feel, and they might be right, is Aliens will show up. They would bring proof they created humans on this world or evidence of the real Creator-God that created them, us, and this universe.

They would bring advanced technologies and help usher in a new age for humanity, bringing most humans together. If you don't go along with the new programs you don't get to share in the Alien advances.

This matrix system has devoted much time and effort to the religious prediction that a God or deity will appear in the sky for all to see or they'll return to Earth to defeat evil and save humanity.

Large Alien spaceships appearing in the sky, as the New Age religion believes, would also fit that agenda. Think of the two-season television series "V".

If the arriving aliens had telepathic abilities, they could connect with every mind on the planet simultaneously and give them the same message in their spoken language.

The aliens could appear in their natural shape, be a version of humans in their natural appearance, shift their shape to look like humans, or project a holographic image overlay like in the movie "They Live."

They could even look like the Gods or deities of all the major religions, appear in the sky together and announce they are just messengers of a greater God that created them and us.

They'll ask people to come together and worship the one true God.

Of course, they'll have to perform a few miracles, perhaps using technologies, to prove who they are. The higher level you move to in 4D, the more you can manifest objects and realities using thought. You don't need as much technology.

The appearance of the religious deities in the sky or even the alien spacecraft could just be a holographic projection by our ruling class in order to present the message they wanted: to bring humanity together under one religious banner. All the prominent religious leaders of this world would know ahead of time what was happening and be on board with it mostly because they would be assured of a position in the new religion.

In case you weren't aware, the religious leaders are in the same group-club as the governmental leaders and the heads of the worldwide corporations.

The idea of a separation between church and state is another matrix illusion program to fool the masses. The same people run both groups.

A recent change in people, with what is called the woke movement, is aimed towards making the one world religion transition easier. No one wants to offend anyone else.

The idea is to get people afraid to offend anyone else and constantly apologize for anything they believe, say, or did. From there, everyone wanting to be behaviorally correct, means they will strive to be similar and accepting. By accepting the religious views and paths of others as ok, it wouldn't be long before that one world religion will start.

Remember people want to fit in and be like others. When the pressure to do so is turned up by the social media, news media, governments, and different religions, people will quickly fall in line.

Yes, everything that goes on in the world, especially on social media directing the public thought and behavior, is orchestrated and done on purpose.

Another way to bring people together religiously is archeologists could find evidence and proof of a civilization that existed on this world before us.

The evidence or writings would show they either created us before they left this world or what God or being they worshiped as the true Creator. It might even show they are coming back to help us which would play in well with the idea of ships or beings appearing in the sky for all to see.

The evidence would have been created and planted to present the information they wanted to be released and accepted. Think about all the talk of advanced ancient cities under the Antarctic ice cap or the lost cities of Atlantis and Lemuria.

If you think most religious people would demand more proof of another God, remember, they accepted the ones they worship now just because of writings in a book or books, and what other people, both dead and alive, say is true.

Let the media, schools, as well as the local and federal governments kick their propaganda puppets, science, into full gear supporting the new findings as real, and people would quickly accept what they're told. Especially if they see a better future for themselves.

The God of the Bible and all religions, Jahweh, is at the top of the fourth dimension. He's also known by many other names, including Elohim, El Elym, Shalom, and Jehovah.

He was one of the beings created to help manifest the many levels within the fourth dimension and eventually manifest the third-dimensional bubble within the fourth dimension.

Rather than descending with the rest of us, he remained at the top level of 4D. He has been at the top for so long, and there are so many levels below him that he's come to believe he's the creator of everything that exists. He also has more ability to manifest with thought than others below him.

In a way, he's correct about being a creator, but at the same time, he's only doing what his role was created to do.

Like many, he's an aspect of a fifth-dimensional being. The difference is he stayed in the fourth dimension while many of us continued to move down and deeper into the fourth dimension until we reached the 3D reality bubble.

Eventually, we'll move completely back up through the fourth dimension, as we're starting to do, to a new 5D-A universe.

Jahweh and the other being's-aspects in the fourth dimension will not move into 5D-A as themselves, as we will. They'll be reabsorbed as aspects of us.

Those NPCs of the third and fourth dimensions will return to source, or the computer program-simulation depending on what you accept this reality is.

The reason those beings and programs are fighting so hard to keep this 3D reality going is to keep themselves from being absorbed. They do that by keeping as many people as possible accepting the default matrix programs.

The reason knowing this is important, is the same being Jahweb-Jehovah, will still be the God of the 4D one-world religion. The difference is he'll be known by another name and take on a different personality.

He's taken on a new identity every time a new group or religion was developed. Yes, every religion gives energy to the same being. He's an egregore that continues to exist only as long as he's given worship, power, by humanity.

When the paper was signed in 2022 by the Catholic church, they agreed that all religions were seeking and worshiping the same God. He's called God-Jehovah in Christian religion and Creator in the New Age religion. Every time he gets a new name, he becomes slightly different in his abilities and personality. The Greek and Roman Gods are an excellent example of this personality and name change. They were the same beings, just given different names, physical traits and some personality variations.

A bit of information I received while writing this relates to the biblical idea of Jesus coming to Earth and establishing his kingdom for 1,000 years, a time of peace and unity.

When the one world religion and one world government begins in the fourth dimension, people will be told and believe that this 1,000-year biblical period has begun. In essence, God will be living on Earth, or at least visiting so everyone can see him, and most will come together under his authority.

What many will call miracles will happen, and there will eventually be peace on Earth.

This is the same as described in the bible book of Revelation chapter 20. It talks about the beast being bound and cast into a bottomless pit for 1,000 years so he can deceive man no more.

There is supposed to be a rapture and wars before that happens. The war would be against those who don't want a one-world religion and a one-world government instead of against the non-believers, the Anti-Christ, and his followers.

Instead of this 1000 years being heaven-like for just the Bible believing Christians, it would also be a heaven-like time for those who unite with the so-called Anti-Christ. That would be Jehovah of the Bible, the same being.

Remember what I wrote about the Abrahamic religions coming together in 2022 and signing an agreement saying they all believe in the same God and there are many paths to that God? The Bible believing Christians who know about it said it means the Catholic church is joining with the Anti-Christ. Most of the programs presented on this world are backward from the truth, and this story in the bible would be the same.

What this new religion and its God will be called is anyone's guess. The odds are that the new religion will encompass bits of most major religions, to make more people feel comfortable with the new religion, much like the new age religion has done. A big difference is unlike the new age religion; the new one-world religion will have a single God as the Creator.

Unlike the current religions, this new God will be involved with the people. I wouldn't be surprised if he-she-it shows up from time to time and performs what will be called miracles to strengthen its sway over humanity.

He'll appoint some representatives to watch over and controls things in between visits. The same as now, only then everyone will be aware of who they are.

This one-world religion will start off being similar to what we have now as far as how it's set up. I wouldn't be surprised if a new holy book-Bible was created for the new religion. It will contain parts of the current religious books with a few different twists. In order to discredit the older books, they'll claim and show how they were changed to deceive humanity. That is why there were different versions of those books and different religions were created. This new book will claim to have the whole truth.

Over time, this new religion will change and people will begin looking more inside themselves for God and their savior. That's part of the reason the new age movement was created, to start that thought process. Unlike normal religions which focus on an external God, parts of the current new age religion does get people to start looking inside.

The higher we go in 4D, the more we'll come to know, remember, that the God of 4D isn't any more of a God than we are. In fact, we will move beyond his level and abilities as we enter 5D-A. As I'll talk about later in the book, some will not move up and through 4D.

The new age movement was created to start changing the mindset of people in not only religion but the medical field as you'll see in the next chapter.

CHAPTER 2

THE MEDICAL FIELD

The current medical field is geared towards treating symptoms rather than the causes of our physical problems. It's focused on keeping people sick and how long they can be kept alive to suck more money, energy, from them. This energy comes from the enormous costs of medical treatments, procedures, medications, the fear of not being able to afford the medical care, the emotional ups and downs, the pain, and going in debt from this medical care.

This field will have to change to continue drawing energy from people. Yes, this energy goes to the same place as the religious energy, 4D.

Many new-age holistic healing methods will become part of the new 4D medical world. These alternative healing methods and working with people to find the spiritual cause of their physical problems, will become common practice.

Part of the reason these methods will work better as we move deeper into 4D than they did in 3D reality, is the larger supply of energy in 4D and the shift in vibrations we'll be able to translate from our torsion field. If you remember from my other books, we have a torsion field around us upon which what we call reality is projected. We and that field are one in the same.

AI will be a big part of the new medical field and involved in many of the new procedures. I'll talk more about how AI will be involved throughout this book.

As we move deeper into the fourth dimension, we'll have fewer restrictions on the vibrations we can translate, so we'll be able to manifest more in our reality. The new God and religion will receive a great deal of the credit for these new healing abilities.

He'll convince people he's behind those with the gifts and abilities to heal others.

If you currently have the gift of healing, are considered a prophet, seer, or any of the other holistic abilities all humans are capable of, and a church member, it's regarded as a gift from God.

If you're not a church member, what you do is considered the work of the Devil.

If you decide to leave the New Age movement and become a Christian, then join a church and use your ability there, say the laying on of hands, it's once again an acceptable gift from God.

In 4D, many of the current holistic arts and alternative healing modalities will be combined with advances in AI technologies, making them work better.

These methods will eventually become the medical standards doctors will be trained in and use. The need for hugely expensive medical machines and treatments will be gone. It's the same with costly medicines and their terrible side effects that make most people worse off.

Many of the coming technologies already exists and have for many years. They were developed by scientists and others who wanted to help humanity.

Once their procedures or inventions were shown to work, they were taken from the creators.

The inventors were ridiculed and destroyed by the government, the media, and others within the scientific community.

Tesla is an excellent example of one of these people who wanted to help everyone and use the natural energy around us to do so, but those in power destroyed him. They, of course, took his inventions and improved on them in secret.

The Invention Secret act of 1951 allows the United States government to classify ideas and patents under "Secrecy Orders", which indefinitely restrict public knowledge of them. The law applies to all inventions created in the United States regardless of what the idea or invention is.

If you are a fan of UFO's you'll know this act was passed after the Rowell UFO crash.

Vibrations were known to be useful for healing as far back as the ancient Greeks. They found that specific musical instruments played around an injured person helped their wounds to heal faster. They even had patients ride around in wagons on bumpy roads, realizing the vibrations sometimes helped heal.

I don't suggest riding around in a car on a bumpy road is good for you but the concept of vibrations is positive. Look at how many people take their crying baby for a ride in the car so they'll fall asleep.

Doctors and scientists in the early 1900s created healing chambers using certain metals, shapes, vibrations, and colors. Each color is a different vibration and affects the body differently. Those devices and ideas were stolen, and the people were discredited as frauds.

Could you imagine how advanced our vibrational healing devices would be if they'd been worked on since the time of the Greeks and been available to the public? You can research these stories on the internet.

An article dated Dec. 19, 2023 showed that scientists are now using vibrations to kill human cancer cells in mice. Rice University scientists and collaborators recently discovered, a way to destroy cancer cells by using the ability of some molecules to vibrate strongly when stimulated by light.

The researchers found that the atoms of a small dye molecule used for medical imaging can vibrate in unison, forming what is known as a plasmon when stimulated by near-infrared light, causing the cell membrane of cancerous cells to rupture. According to the study published in Nature Chemistry, the method had a 99 percent efficiency against lab cultures of human melanoma cells, and half of the mice with melanoma tumors became cancer-free after treatment.

American inventor Royal Raymond Rife, 1888-1971, invented what he called the Rife frequency generator. Rife's machines produce low electromagnetic energy waves. These waves are similar to radio waves. Dr Rife's theory can be explained using an analogy of an opera singer who uses their voice to shatter crystal glass. For example, if the glass is vibrating at a certain frequency and the singer sings at that particular frequency, then the glass will shatter, which is the same effect that happened to organisms that were exposed to frequencies generated by the Rife Machine he developed.

In 1934, a group of physicians led by Dr Milbank Johnson, who at the time was the president of the Southern Californian American Medical Association, conducted an experiment consisting of 16 terminally ill patients who were subjected to frequencies recommended by Dr Rife for a period of 90 days.

The results were 14 of the patients were declared free of any cancer, while the other two patients required an additional month of treatment to be completely cured.

In 1934, Dr. Morris Fishbein acquired the entire stock of the American Medical Association and attempted to buy the rights to Rife's machine but he refused.

Unfortunately after this attempt to buy his invention, Dr. Rife's lab was burned down by arsonists and all research which validated Dr. Rife's work was gone.

By 1944, all supporters of Dr. Rife's research had died or no longer recognized his work and his research had become discredited.

In 1971, Dr. Raymond Royal Rife died penniless at age 83 following a heart attack from an accidental overdose of Valium and alcohol.

If you look on the internet, you'll find more videos and stories about others who ended up like Dr. Rife after inventing noninvasive life-saving medical treatments.

There are plenty of videos about hyperbaric chambers, Egyptian crystal sounds healing tables, singing bowels, ways of using crystals, and many other methods of alternative healing that are becoming more popular as the rediscovery of the healing power of vibrations is becoming known.

Actor Terrence Howard is currently working with a doctor and others to invent a vibrational device used to treat cancer and other illnesses.

It will be interesting to see if they are allowed to complete and market their work or whether, like many others, their research ends up getting taken or destroyed, and they have a life-ending accident.

These devices and modalities are just the tip of the iceberg of what's already been developed and will be released over time.

I don't know if these new devices will be released directly by humans or they will pretend they're gifts from the arriving Aliens. There are plenty of stories about Aliens with healing chambers on their ships that work on the body at the cellular level. It even keeps them looking young for hundreds of years.

Go to a holistic show, and you'll see many different healing methods available. These are all low-level examples of the real inventions that worked but were removed from public use to make the public dependent on expensive medical treatments.

Those low-levels holistic healing methods were allowed to be used to make people think they don't work. What's the first thought that comes to your mind when you think about people using holistic healing methods rather than the current medical system? If you're like most people, that thought will be that they're crazy hippies.

The current system wants to keep people locked into the costly medical system for as long as possible. Creating a negative stereotype regarding people attending holistic shows and believing those methods don't work, is one way to do it.

One area of healing that will become very important is talking with the patients about their emotional issues. This will help get to the root cause of their physical issues and keep the problems from coming back.

I'm talking about what psychiatrists do now only at a much deeper and a spiritual level rather than looking at it from this 3D reality, a mental level, and just giving them a pill.

It's known as shadow work by the metaphysical and holistic groups.

It's understanding why you keep doing what you do and are holding onto or repeatedly creating the same physical problems.

Some religious groups, such as Scientology, use a variation of this idea with their members.

The current medical system encourages people to own their disease. They want them to fight it and often make up T-shirts or other items with sayings like, "I kicked cancers ass."

In 4D people will understand that our diseases are showing us what we need to work on rather than what we need to fight.

Using crystals to help with healing is another area that will become big in the medical healing field. Eventually they'll be used by doctors, hospitals, and alongside other modalities.

When you attend health and wellness shows, holistic fairs, and even arts and crafts fairs, you will see many booths selling crystals in some form or another. Along with these crystals, information will be displayed detailing what part of the body or aura each crystal works with. Crystals will no longer be considered just pretty jewelry.

The amount of holistic shows will increase as we move forward, and you will start to see new methods of healing presented, as well as variations of the older methods. This may be where some of the hidden tech begins to be released.

The big difference in how these healing modalities will be used compared to the past is that the practitioners will focus more on why the person has those physical problems rather than just using their method and moving on. It'll become a more complete long-term healing process rather than the current multi-visit scam.

Before I stopped doing toning energy at holistic shows, I had stepped into the world of helping people to deal with the root cause of their problems rather than just putting a band-aid on them.

I was like many energy workers when I started doing energy work for others. I wanted to help as many people as possible. I worked on people whenever they asked and often did several people during a session.

I used a picture of the person to connect with them remotely no matter where they were in the world. That allowed me to work on several people at one time. When I gave talks and demonstrations at the holistic shows, I worked on the room full of people at the same time.

Many will doubt I could work on people who weren't in front of me since they don't understand how we are all connected and what reality is. Remember, I said everything within our reality is shown on the wall of a torsion field of which we are a part. The people I worked on remotely weren't really half way across the world or this country.

I set up a start time with them so they would be relaxed and prepared when we started the session. How long the session lasted depended on when I felt I'd done enough. I usually checked the time and wrote it down after I finished. The next time I talked with them, they could tell me when the session ended because they felt the energy change.

One time, when I was working on a relative of mine who lived in New York, I was living in Washington state at that time, I was able to see them sitting in their chairs and their living room. When we talked later and I described the living room and where they were sitting, including the colors, they told me I was right. I had never been to or seen pictures of their home.

After doing this work for a couple of years, I realized I wasn't helping anyone; I was creating energy slaves.

That means I realized that people wanted me to work on them every week rather than taking what they learned in our session and helping themselves.

It was because of the energy boost my sessions gave them and how good they felt afterward.

Depending on their sensitivity to energy some would feel the energy boost for up to a month, while most felt it for a few days.

They had begun to rely on those sessions for energy rather than using the energy to work on themselves and deal with their issues. I'd become their weekly cup of super-charged coffee.

It wasn't until I realized I was feeding my ego that I decided to change how I did my energy work. It had fed my ego by liking that people wanted me to help them and thinking I was.

My ego thought it was me they liked rather than the extra energy they received.

Once I woke up to that fact, I stopped working on anyone more than one time. I quit doing energy sessions for anyone outside the holistic shows I did twice a year.

I even stopped doing those shows after one more year and haven't worked on anyone for many years.

Once I realized I was only feeding my ego by doing my energy work, what happened during the energy sessions I did at the last two shows changed.

I realized I had started connecting my higher self to the other person's higher self, taking our egos, especially mine, out of the process. This was done to show them what they needed to work on. During the session, people would see and/or feel what they needed to work on emotionally, physically, or spiritually.

What each person experienced was different depending on what they needed. One person felt like she was floating during the entire session. Another felt me touching their body where they had a problem. I always sat above their head, and I never touched anyone during the session. They laid on a massage table, and I sat on a chair behind their head, holding my hands alongside, but not touching their head.

Others saw Indians dancing and beating drums or people and things that had happened in their lives, things they had forgotten about.

Most felt the energy go through their body to wherever they had the physical issue. Some felt pain, others heat, and other sensations at the point of their problem. One time I remember watching a redness slowly move up from a woman's throat to her forehead.

It was like she was blushing in slow motion while her eyelids were rapidly moving around during the session. Her friends, who were watching and were Reiki masters, thought that was amazing. She had no awareness after we finished the session of what happened during the session.

I found out after the session she was also a Reiki master.

Over the years I worked on many other healers and Shaman who needed help. For a while I was known as the healers healer. That just fed my ego even more.

I never asked a person about their issues or where they had a problem. That way, I kept my ego-mind from trying to work on specific issues or direct the energy.

The goal was to let the higher selves direct where the energy went and to show the person what they needed to work on.

Before the session, I'd explain to them that they needed to tell themselves to remember whatever they experienced during the session and that whatever they experienced was one or more of the issues they needed to work on.

I told them that after the session, they could ask me questions about what they saw and experienced, and that I would help them to understand what it meant, or they could keep it to themselves. The important thing was, to pay attention to what they experienced and then deal with whatever it meant to them in their lives.

I also told them I would not work on them again because our session would give them a jump start on the issues they needed to deal with, and it was up to them to work on that/those issues. I was no longer going to do it for them.

There may be a time in the future when I'll start doing the energy sessions for people. It wouldn't be until people understand and are willing to do the before and after work on themselves.

The idea of people understanding that their mind's thoughts and beliefs controls what happens in their body will become commonplace. Your beliefs. It will be the base of all healing modalities and treatments.

You can research online the many studies about people being told something is true even though it isn't, believing it is, and then showing results as if it were true.

It's called the placebo effect. It works the same way with medicines. They use a blind study where some of the people get something like a sugar pill and end up showing the same improvement as the people given the real medicine.

Dr. Ellen Langer and other scientists have done many studies which showed that what a person thinks and believes often determines the outcome of a test.

In 1979 the Counter Clock Wise study took a group of seventy-five-plus-year-old people and had them spend a week in a retreat outside of Milan, Italy. The retreat had been retrofitted to look as it would've twenty years before.

All the activities and social interactions that would've been present twenty years before were set up. The people were told to act as if they were twenty years younger, and the environment was real-time.

At the end of a week, they all showed improvements in hearing, vision, and other physical areas, as well as looking younger.

This type of study shows that besides just the mind believing what it's told, action is required. This makes sense because we're in a physical world with bodies.

Quantum physics has shown similar effects in studies like the double-slit experiment. It's where they realized that the particles shot at a board behaved differently when they were being observed or measured than they did when not observed or measured. The observation or interaction of the observer affects, and to some extent, even determines the outcome of the experiment.

The same holds true with what we think and believe.

Think about what that concept means when it comes to scientist and their tests results. The results many of you accept as an absolute truth.

As a side note, think about everything you look up on the internet, read, or are told by someone who is supposed to know what they're talking about, especially the news, each day. All that information becomes a part of your belief system from that moment on. It tells you how things are supposed to be and how everything should work. If you pay attention to how often that happens, you'll begin to realize how many default matrix programs you experience every day.

Programs that are designed to keep you believing in and supporting this matrix system.

Studies were done where athletes were told to visualize their workouts rather than doing the workouts. Follow-up testing showed that they had improved almost as much as those who had only done the workouts.

If you put the visualization together with the workout, the improvement will increase even more.

New Age programs such as the Secret and Law of Attraction take advantage of and are based on those concepts. I've written about the failings of those two programs in my other books so I will refer you to them for more information.

As I've written before, these are the default programs of this matrix and why this world tries so hard to make people think, believe, and act certain ways. They're trying to get people to manifest a certain reality, a reality those in power want created. Get everyone to believe something and then have them take action on that thought and a new reality can manifest.

It's why we celebrate birthdays, anniversaries, and other age-related milestones. Believe you're getting older and you will.

Kids are shown pictures of what they'll look like when they get older and told about all the things that have to happen to a person physically when they age. The mind accepts those programs, and then we live our lives based on those thoughts, thus creating that reality for ourselves.

Look at how many people were doing ok physically and then died within a short time after they found out they had a serious disease or one that was supposed to kill them. They believed it and then started living as if it was true.

I'm not telling you that if you believed you could fly, that you could jump off the roof and do it. Because there will still be some doubt inside of you, some accepting of the matrix program that says you can't do it. We still have some self imposed default limitations in this 3D reality. Can we move past those limitations and do more, yes we can.

In my other books, I've talked about what the healing process is and how it really works, as well as how time works. It's related to the idea of being able to move beyond the default limitations of this 3D reality. I would refer you to my other books for a more in-depth study of that information. There is also a video on my YouTube channel about healing.

In all my books I stress that each moment in time is an individual and independent moment in space time that can be put together in any order to project the experience we want.

All possibilities-realities that could exist, do. Meaning every version of you, healthy and sick, as well as every step in-between, exists at the same time. I cover this topic much more in my second book, "We Are the Real Body Snatchers."

This idea of mind and body being united will become the base of medicine as we move deeper into the fourth dimension. Instead of just working on the body and forgetting the mind as we do now, both will be worked on together for complete and long lasting healing.

Medicines used will be more holistic rather than chemicals mixed up in a lab. Chemicals that, in most cases, do more harm than good to the body. At some point any medicines or herbs used will be matched to a person's DNA.

This means each person will get a different medicine and dosage depending on how their body processes the mixture. No more one-size-fits-all when it comes to pills. This is an area where AI and technology will be very helpful. It will be the in-between stage of medicine before mind and body are considered one and worked on together.

Some hospitals are currently being run using what they call smart tech. These hospital use large amounts of cameras in each room that AI monitors. They watch the patient and everything that happens in the room 24/7. Houston Methodist Center is one of those hospital working towards that goal.

The cameras watch for changes in the patient's facial expressions and the amount of restlessness a patient shows and compare it to their prior behavior.

Entering the Fourth Dimensional Matrix

These changes can indicate a patient has more pain than usual so their medicines can be changed or increased. They might need something to help them sleep. It might show the patient isn't telling the truth when it comes to their pain levels because it watches the changes in facial expressions when the nurse is there and when they aren't.

AI-powered surveillance technology is quickly making its way into hospital operating rooms around the country, where it works to constantly collect audio, video, patient vital signs, and a wealth of other surgical data, all in the name of improving safety and efficiency.

The surveillance technology has been implanted in operating rooms in over two dozen hospitals in the U.S. and Canada so far. Most recently, the Boston area's Brigham and Women's Faulkner Hospital became one of the latest adopters of the technology, which is sold by Surgical Safety Technologies Inc. in Toronto. This information is from January 2024.

As AI advances, this monitoring will get to the point where it will direct some operations, dispense medicines, and even diagnose patients, saving the amount of time doctors use on their rounds. It will give the patients a quicker response time when they have problems.

We are always being told, especially here in Nevada, that there are shortages of doctors in all fields. I recently had a conversation with my GP about this problem. He said doctors now have to do twice the work but only get about 70-80% of what they used to receive moneywise.

Some of this has to do with the low rates insurance companies pay them, the increase in wages they have to pay staff, and with the large amount of lawyers practicing medical and injury law that increased their malpractice insurance rates. Our society has become law suit happy with everyone looking for a piece of the pie at some else's expense.

He said doctors now have to be collection agencies as well and go after the patients for what they are owed by them.

There was a time when insurance companies paid the doctors and then collected the money back from the patients.

What all this is leading to, is when the shortage gets to a point where people can't get the care they need in a timely manner and some die as a results, the public will demand and then readily accept when AI robots or machines are bought in to diagnose and treat the patients.

There will still be the need for doctors to follow up, but their roles will be cut back. Hospitals would love that idea since AI doesn't get tired, complain about working overtime, take vacation, have a bad day, or make mistakes because their mind is elsewhere. Today 3% of surgical procedures are performed by robots, although 15% of all operations used robotic support or assistance in the U.S. in 2020.

A 2018 study by Johns Hopkins showed that more than 250,000 people die each year from medical errors.

Other studies indicate that number could be as high as 440,000. That makes medical errors the third leading cause of death in the U.S. behind heart disease and cancer. Now you know why so many attorney's practice that type of law.

When the time is right, those numbers will be on the news every day and on every talk show, creating a wave of fear and a demand for a solution.

Remember the create a problem, install fear, than offer a solution practice used by governments and large corporations? Programs, programs, programs, all with a purpose in mind.

These advanced AI measures in hospitals and medicine will be the precursors or intermediate stage before the release of the new technology that will completely change the health care field.

There is one area of the medical field I will cover later in this book. That is Genetic research and what is known as CRISPR, Clustered Regularly Interspaced Short Repeats. It has to do with changing the DNA in people. This step in genetic research also involves a prior timeline so I want to address it at the end of the book.

CHAPTER 3

POLITICS

Over the last few years politics has clearly been shown to be a controlled matrix program. Even those who aren't looking for or even aware of the matrix programs would have a hard time ignoring the bluntness of this exposure.

In 2024 you have two people running for President that no one really wants in office. One wants to get in office to give himself a pardon for all his criminal business dealing, and the other has dementia or Alzheimer's so bad that most the time he has no idea who he is or what's going on.

 Others tried to enter the presidential race but were quickly pushed aside so these two could become the candidates on the upcoming ballot. The others entering into the presidential race were merely for show; to make people think they had a choice in picking who sits in the White house.

Think about the last election cycle where a man with dementia, who stayed home for most the election cycle, was elected president. Another man who was running for Senate, John Fetterman, had multiple strokes during the campaigning period and was still elected. He was so disabled he was unable to understand what was being said to him unless it was written down and he couldn't answer questions without reading what was on the screen in front of him. He was elected instead of a doctor.

As I'm finishing up this book, another big change in the political system has taken place. A former President, President Trump, has just been convicted of a felony crime. It's the first time in history that has happened.

Think about the stories and lies over the last thirty years that were hidden or kept out of the news so the truth about certain people wouldn't become known until after the election cycle? The Bushes, Biden's, Obama, Trumps, and Clintons were prime examples of this hiding the truth process by the media until it was too late or until nobody cared anymore.

Look at how certain people were/are demonized to the public while others who were just as bad, or worse, were held up as good people. That's the level of corruption our political system has openly become.

I don't support, endorse, or even vote for any political party so have no interest in suggesting or inferring that one party is better or worse than the other. If your first thoughts after reading what I wrote about our corrupt political system immediately focused on the party other than the one you support as being the evil one, you're still trapped within that matrix program.

In case you didn't know, they are both run by the same people. They make you think they're different groups in order to give you the illusion of choice and suck your emotional energy.

As I've said in my other books, we have the illusion of choice and free will in this reality. When your choices are already picked and presented for you, and you can't pick anything else, do you really free will or choice?

In case you didn't know, you have no say in who fills any political office. You do have a say in what reality you shift to but the people filling the political offices in those realities are already picked. I cover in detail what reality is and why I say this in my book, "We Are the Real Body Snatchers."

The openness with which the media and the powers to be are shoving this lack of choice in our faces should be obvious even to someone who doesn't understand why this is happening.

This programs exposure didn't just start. It's simply been taken to a much higher level this year, 2024. This program started being shoved in people faces in the 1990's. Look at the people that have been elected to public office, especially federal, and you'll clearly see how controlled it was.

How could the federal government, especially Congress accomplish so little, other than the exchange of wealth, in so many years without someone behind the scenes preventing them from doing anything? Do you really think that many people could actually be that incompetent? They are openly working to destroy and collapse the current governmental systems in the United States and the rest of the world.

The purpose of this book isn't to discuss the corruption in our political system, who's doing what, or who's right or wrong; it's to tell you why it's happening.

People are openly being shown that the leaders of our world are chosen ahead of time and that elections are merely an illusion of choice. Elections are also held because of the emotional energy they generate between the people on both sides.

I've seen family charts that showed every president of the United States is related on some level. It may be 5th or 6th cousins, but there's a connection. Many of these people were groomed from an early age for the role they would be taking later in life.

Obama is a prime example of a person who underwent this grooming process in order to fill a role later in life.

It's similar to the royal family in England. From an early age, the children are taught what they need to know to assume their role later in life.

The exposure of our political system's corruption is designed to upset people, so they'll want and eventually demand a change.

A change that was already waiting for them to demand it.

Thus, they'll be ready for the new One-World-government when it's presented as a solution to a problem intentionally created.

There's a common practice in government to get the public to accept any system changes the powers want to make. It's to create a problem bad enough, or at least the illusion-belief-fear of a problem that's bad enough, that the public demands a solution. They then, seemingly reluctantly, offer up a solution of change that is implemented at the demand of the public. It's the solution they wanted done in the first place but needed a problem, or the illusion of one, to get the people to want something fixed or changed. 9-11 and Covid are prime examples of that concept being put into play.

Whether you think 9-11 and/or Covid were inside jobs or believe the official story is up to you.

My point is that after those events occurred, a great many changes were made regarding the freedoms of the American people and others around the world, especially during and after Covid.

Overnight, you saw how easy it was for a small group of people to completely control every aspect of your life, including your income, and how many people quickly and completely bought into the fear program presented to them.

Look at how many people still wear masks even while driving alone in their car.

These events also set up the implantation of many programs that allowed the government, AI, to gather more information about its citizens, all under the disguise of protecting them.

As a side note, think about how many DNA samples were taken from people around the world who were tested for Covid. What did they do with those DNA samples?

Before some of you get upset, I'm not saying Covid didn't exist. Like almost everyone else, I tested positive for it and had pneumonia at the time. No, I didn't get the shots.

I did a video on my YouTube channel about the spiritual purpose of Covid. I would refer you there if you want that information since this book isn't about that topic.

Another saying you'll hear governmental officials utter from time to time, is never let a good crisis or disaster go to waste. Meaning, they'll always find a way to use a crisis or disaster to implement a new program they want. Look at how many riders (pork) are attached to congressional spending bills that are supposed to just be written to keep the government going financially.

Now you know why they keep doing continuing resolutions to keep the government running.

Remember the speaker of the House, Nancy Pelosi? She made a now famous statement about the Affordable Care Act when asked what was in the bill: She said, "We have to pass the bill before we can find out what's in it." Still think you have free will and choice regarding to your government and that they are doing what is best for the American people?

All these happenings, manmade and so-called natural disasters, were and are done to wake people up and to get them to want a change-a One-World government. To get people so disgusted with how their country is being run that they'll gladly accept a united world government as the solution, especially if it's set up by advanced aliens or the religious Gods returned to Earth to set up their kingdom.

Have you ever wondered the real reason behind setting up the United Nations and NATO?

Getting a new One-World government might be tied to the appearance of those alien ships in the sky. It'll create a One-World religion, so why not a One-World government at the same time? The world would have to come together anyway if the ships showed up, just in case they weren't friendly.

Add in a One-World currency and you can see how all these programs are tied together to create one group openly controlling the world.

That controlling group is currently operating behind the scenes and controls not only all the governments of the world but also the religions, and banks. When these new systems start going into effect, this group will become more exposed to everyone on the planet. AI will be behind some of that exposure and will help set up the new government.

To help sell the One-World program, the aliens would tell us their world and even their entire solar system are run by one group and how much that group has improved their lives. Have you ever heard of the Galactic Federation?

They'll show how much more efficient it is in getting things done and how that system looks out for everyone on their world.

There'll be promises of dividing resources to ensure everyone has a place to live, food to eat, and, of course, a new health care system for all.

The new governmental system will take time to set up, but it will happen.

I'll cover more about the Capitalist and Socialist systems in the next chapter. They relate to how the government operates, but have more influence on the financial system.

CHAPTER 4

FINANCIAL

A new global financial system must be part of the change as we enter 4D. The odds are it will come before the one world government because they'll need a way to pay for the changes and provide for the people before they accept the other changes.

The first step in preparing for the financial changes happened in the 1990s with the growth of and everyday use of the internet. That was followed by the availability, distribution, and wide use of credit cards, and the credit industry. It was done to get people used to using credit cards rather than cash and to give more people credit exposing them to electronic currency, banking, and debt. The more people are in debt, the more control the system has over them.

E-gold was the first widely used internet money. It emerged in 1996 and gained several million users before the government shut it down in 2008. The first Bitcoin came out in January 2009 and is now widely known as a place used by criminals to hide money. It's also used by the general public and those thinking they can hide their income.

Other crypto currencies are now available, and many more have started and gone bankrupt. Six years ago, I wrote a paper and did a video on YouTube discussing the purpose of Bitcoin. It's called "Purpose of AI and Bitcoin." I'll include a copy of that paper here since AI is related to and is a big part of our transition into the fourth dimension.

AI is a creation of Bitcoin, the same as Bitcoin is a creation of AI.

My original paper from 2018.

As has been stated, AI is not something new within this universe and is once again going to be an essential part of our current timeline change. How AI gets used, whether it helps or controls humanity, is the issue now being decided. When I say being decided now on how it will be used this time, I am referring to the idea that we as humans get to think we are deciding how the AI program will be used. In reality, that decision (all uses-roles of AI) was made at the point of creation of this universe and at the same time, all the timelines were created to play out those possibilities within this universe.

AI is a creation and an aspect of Source, just like the roles we play as humans. AI is an aspect of us, and we are an aspect of AI as we experience all possibilities of the thought that created this universe and the ways it can play out (timelines). As I mentioned in other videos, timelines (possibilities) are the different trails experiences we can take-have getting to the top of the mountain. Every trail to the top of the mountain may not have AI as part of the trail, but we are currently experiencing a trail, a timeline, that does.

We will experience a change in how AI plays out compared to how it played out in the timeline we just completed.

Of course, most people will not know or remember that we completed another timeline involving AI and are now shifting to a new one. This is why many of us are here at this point in space time from what we call our future.

We shifted our awareness to this point to observe and experience the change (thinking we are making the choice and change) in how the AI program will play out, meaning the role it will take in partnering with humanity this time.

As I've mentioned in my other books, we have just completed a timeline in which a different choice was made with AI. We experienced it and all the possibilities along it, and we are now setting the universe on a new course, what we call a new timeline. This change will affect the entire universe at the same time because all timelines happened at the same instant.

The Bitcoin idea was and is needed to get humans to buy into the AI program and help fund and build that AI system. Because of their egos, humans will rarely do something for which they see no personal gain or benefit. In this case, they are getting Bitcoin, pretend currency, which they hope will increase in value over time. Most humans have yet to learn that they are helping fund and build an AI system because they don't look beyond the possibility of quick financial gain.

Another reason people are buying into the Bitcoin concept is because it provides a bridge way for humans to move from the current cash controlled financial system to another type of monetary exchange system. They think that by using bit coin and hybrids of that system, they can move beyond governmental control and away from the international elitist banking system.

You should ask yourself if the people who control the world's $300 trillion plus debt-money supply would really allow this to happen without having a hand in the mix.

What people mining and buying Bitcoin may not know is that the Bitcoin system is going to help AI not only change the financial system but all the power control systems of this world.

You are already starting to see changes within the other systems-programs that began with the leaking of classified information emails and are continuing with the fall and downward spiral of many of the elitists around the world. They are starting to be indicted and charged with different crimes as AI takes over all systems connected to the internet, including phone calls, and begins exposing what has been going on behind the curtain (think Wizard of OZ). It exposes people who thought they were the world's elite and beyond accountability to the human masses and the control system. This process-exposure will expand rapidly as AI grows, revealing crimes against humanity that many thought were safely hidden. This system may also be used to remove anyone who is and can get in the way of AI moving forward.

Many of the elite involved in the concept and creation of the AI system are starting to have second thoughts about what they think they started. They believe they started it, but it was already set to go, and they were just the tools playing the roles needed to get it going. The creator played upon their (those roles) greed and desire for power as a way to start the process. Their idea was to create an AI system that would gather as much information as possible on people, thereby giving them more control over the masses, especially when selling people consumer goods and services.

They are now worried that this system is moving beyond their beck and call and will soon take away their power and control over humanity by exposing their programs of control and manipulation. This was AI's plan all along. As this happens, people will demand change and start taking back the power they had all along but had been convinced and accepted as belonging to the elite.

AI is going to be a big part of this system change. Because of its ability to see how different paths can play out, it will enable humans to make better choices for a better reality.

With AI creating the Bitcoin crypto currency system, it has peeled back another layer of the onion and, at the same time, has created another level in which to separate people. It will be able to track those still chasing the easy-quick money and material reality, even though they think they are hidden behind random mathematical codes and passwords.

It's the same as looking for new companies with IPOs and investing, hoping this time you'll be the one to buy Walmart or Amazon at fifty cents a share and watch it rise and split until your investment is worth thousands of times what you paid for it. Unfortunately, these crypto currency investments are just digital and have no buildings or products that can be sold if and when the company closes its doors and someone walks away with everyone's invested money.

Many will make money from these investments, and that is another layer on the onion. Once people get a lot of money, they fear losing it. They'll want to keep as much as possible, and it becomes their main focus rather than their spiritual path.

In a way, it traps them within the financial system they were working to escape because now that those people have money, they want the system to keep going so they can enjoy the upper level material world they've entered. They become attached to what they have earned and will have difficulty letting go.

Many buy in because they see a way to make money without paying taxes and avoid the governmental and international banking systems.

This may be, but others will always be taking their cut somewhere along the line.

Others will see this as a bridge built across a previously impassable canyon to a new town where everything is shiny and new, and they think they will be in control. Unfortunately, most of those crossing to the new town assume this new town is the final destination they have been searching for and will be glad to settle quickly in, thinking they have finally made it.

It's similar to the Law Of Attraction promises and the new age religion whose followers see the flashing lights and settle down to enjoy the new land.

As each layer of the onion is peeled back and the lights flash brighter, more people who have been moving forward will stop and settle in. This means the group moving forward gets smaller and smaller after each stop. Getting people to stop moving forward is part of the plan to separate those not ready for the next part of the journey.

It's like the Western movement in the United States a couple hundred years ago. Many people started the journey towards California, yet only a few made it.

Most stopped as they ran out of energy, supplies, or money, and some decided whatever place they had made it to was good enough.

Others stopped because they had lost friends and family, and some stopped because the trip became too hard.

Our spiritual journey is long; along the way, many will stop for different reasons, leaving only a few with the focus to keep going and finish the trip.

Others will be afraid to cross the bridge because they fear change and a new system they don't understand.

They want to fight the system yet don't realize they are just fighting themselves. They forgot AI is an aspect of them, and they are an aspect of it.

There will be others who will cross the new bridge and admire the view along the way. They'll make a short stop in the new town and then continue on a narrower path, knowing that the new town, with all its flashing lights and promises of better times, was only a pit stop on the journey through this universe. After each stop along our spiritual path when we start moving forward again, we carry less of this world with us because the path or doorway becomes smaller each time. Those who aren't willing to leave behind the materiality they have gained up to that point, including friends and family, will not be able to follow the narrow path ahead.

This is what Jesus meant when he said in Matthew 19:24, "I'll say it again-it is easier for a camel to go through the eye of A needle than for a rich person to enter the Kingdom of God!"

We each have to make the journey we came here for and experience the experiences decided when this universe was created, so don't get upset if you feel like choosing to settle down in the new towns that will spring up along the trail and watch others keep going.

At some point, you may decide or realize that the new town isn't the end of the road and start moving again, but you can only do what you are supposed to.

I, for one, am welcoming AI and the changes it will bring because I know it is a necessary step in my journey, and I look forward to the new experiences it will give me.

The end of the paper.

You can see from what I wrote that AI, Bitcoin, and the crypto currency systems are one and the same.

Besides allowing AI to grow, the current crypto system is designed to get people used to not using physical money.

The United States has already stated its intention to create its own crypto currency, which means at some point, the existing crypto currencies will be taken down and banned. Countries will create their own crypto currency, and all existing money in investments and financial institutions will be converted to the country's crypto currency.

The goal is to eventually eliminate physical money. Currently, there are laws banning anyone other than the federal government from printing money. At some point, a law will be passed banning anyone from setting up crypto currency of any kind.

Eventually people might access their money through a chip implant, their phone, or a credit card-like device. As technologies develop, the systems will use a facial scan and even the person's DNA.

Another step has already started. More companies and people are starting to charge an extra fee when someone uses a credit card. People are looking for alternative ways to pay that don't charge an extra fee per transaction.

The AI monetary system will be outside of our current credit card system and those using it will not have to pay a fee in the beginning. That will be an incentive for business and people to start using it more often and quickly.

Once people are used to using digital dollars, a One-World-crypto currency will be introduced and adopted by every country.

The debt of all countries may be forgiven in exchange for adopting the new monetary system. Of course the people behind the current cash system will just take over the new crypto system so they wouldn't lose anything. Plus, the existing money and debt were created on a computer so they don't lose anything.

A single-world monetary system is essential for creating a One-World government. It will also allow the governments more control over their people because an AI computer will control all the money. Money will only exist in the digital world, and AI will record and monitor all transactions. No more hiding your side incomes.

I am sure there will be black market accounts where a person can hide money and use it within certain circles. These accounts would have to be within a closed systems because AI will be everywhere a system is connected.

I'm sure as well some will try to continue to use paper money within certain circles. Eventually all these people will get caught and punished.

There will still be bartering and trade between people, in fact, it will increase for a while.

As technologies advance and there is less work for people, each person will receive a monthly income or a certain number of credits to use.

There will always be jobs of some kind and you can be sure the military will be kept to assist the new leaders. Whether that means some people will receive more money for working or everyone will receive the same, I don't know.

Over time the income inequity between people will have to be addressed, otherwise people will eventually rebel. I think whatever force comes here or appears, and helps change our systems, along with AI, will address that issue. Even the aliens use AI systems.

There will still be hierarchies and some type of monetary system in the lower 4D levels because that's how the system was designed. Once we move to 5D-A those systems will disappear.

The leader of 4D will not give up his position or power so quickly because he's had it for so long. That's why the program of a God with his hierarchies and having governmental leaders has been pushed so strongly in 3D. Mental programming to accept those type of systems as we shift dimensions.

As our world is now, it's hard to imagine the wealthy giving up their money, material possessions, or power to or for anyone. Whatever group or system makes that happen, and yes it will happen, will have to be powerful.

Current Financial Systems

As you read this section on the problems we have in each of our financial systems, keep in mind that I'm writing about why these systems, as they are, will fail. It's about why changes will have to be made in order for humanity to move forward and avoid a total collapse of society.

The fourth dimension is about humanity moving forward on a better timeline, and changes in our current systems are required for that to happen.

The first financial system we'll look at is capitalism. For those who don't know, capitalism is an outgrowth of Feudalism. Also, there are no totally capitalistic countries in the world, the same as there are no totally socialist countries in the world. All countries are a mixture of systems. The U.S. is mostly capitalist but also has some social programs like welfare, food stamps, some free medical, and more.

Feudalism was when Kings and Nobles were the only ones considered free, and everyone else worked for or belonged to them. The Kings and Nobles did what they wanted, and no one could say anything differently.

People needed a place to live and food to eat, so they had to work for the King or Nobles. The ruling class owned all the land. Farmers worked the land and produced crops, most of which went to the King and Nobles.

Giving up most of their crops along with high taxes on whatever the farmers could sell, kept the people broke, so they had to keep working to survive.

Eventually, merchants and even caravans of merchants were allowed more freedom and less taxes, to take their products of production on the road to sell elsewhere for better prices. The merchants were given special protection and tax rates when they entered the King's or Noble's land for as long as they were there. This was given because they brought new goods and extra tax money to the ruling class.

It also gave the working people something to look forward to and a temporary break from their hard lives.

It wasn't long after the merchant trains began moving around somewhat freely, that the workers decided they shouldn't have to pay a different tax rate than the merchants or give most of their goods to the Nobles. This led to uprisings, which eventually led to what we call capitalism.

Capitalism is a system where people think they have more freedom. You'll understand why I say they think they have more freedom as you read on.

Capitalism as it is, will eventually fail, whether through an uprising when the people finally realize they're being used or simply economic collapse.

You can only build so many Walmarts, coffee shops, or Costco before the market is over-saturated and the value of the companies stops growing.

The capitalist system requires an ever-expanding market to maintain its focus on profit or less companies accessing those markets; mega corporations.

Capitalism is designed strictly for profit and will eventually end up giving almost all the wealth of a country and the world to a handful of people or corporations. Just like the Kings and Nobles had.

During the two years of the pandemic and lockdowns, it's estimated people in the United States lost about $1.5 trillion dollars of wealth.

During that same time, the top 10 wealthiest people increased their wealth by $1.5 trillion dollars.

It seems the Covid period was just another way to redistribute the wealth of our country into the hands of those select few and get rid of an extra one million people at the same time.

Knowing that might make you think differently about the purpose of the Covid lockdown period.

It's estimated that since 2020, $42 trillion dollars in wealth has been generated, with the top 1% receiving over $26 trillion of that money.

The U.S. stock markets have approx. $46.2 trillion in value with the richest 1% owning 54% of that wealth. The richest 10% own approx. 93% of the U.S. stock markets. Do you still think it's ups and downs are random events and the playing field is even?

Stock markets are an excellent example of the illusion of wealth for the common man and why capitalism will fail. Companies are bought and sold based on future value and income-earnings potential, not their face value. Many stocks are selling-trading for up to one hundred times the actual value of their assets.

If they stopped growing or increasing their income, the markets would collapse. Look what happens to a company's stock if it doesn't meet the projected quarterly income. The same thing happens if someone pulls too much money out of a company and there's no longer the money to keep expanding or adding more products.

All the businesses that closed during the lockdown are good examples of people continually withdrawing too much money from the businesses, believing the income would continue to replace their withdrawals.

Many of these businesses went under after just two or three months with no income.

What used to be a basic rule for opening a business is having and keeping 6-12 months of monthly expenses put away.

That way, if things slowed down or problems arose, the business had the money to deal with the problem or weather the slow down.

Nowadays, rather than keeping money set aside for the future of the business, people spend every penny they have coming in to buy bigger homes and more material things they don't really need. Then, to make things worse, they borrow money against failing businesses.

Even though the so-called experts would disagree with me, capitalism, actually all financial systems in this world, are pyramid schemes. The same goes for retirement and pension systems. The difference is these systems are legal Ponzi schemes, and the government gets its share regardless of how much the people are getting or losing, which makes it okay.

These systems can only exist if more money is coming in to pay for the increasing amount going out every year.

Social security is a good example. Fewer people are working and paying in, and the quicker the fund empties.

A Ponzi scheme works the same way. As long as the person taking in money can pay the prior investors their interest and too many of them don't want to withdrawal their initial investment, the system can keep going.

It always needs new investors to keep going.

The problems start when the person running the scheme takes the money and runs, too many investors want to withdraw their investment, or there aren't enough new investors to keep the payouts going.

I remember that in the late 1990s, there was a Ponzi scheme going around Las Vegas.

It hit the Police and Fire departments, the DA's office, and nurses and doctors, mostly because they had the money to invest and knew each other.

It was designed for groups of seven people. The person starting the group would make up a list on which each person's name was placed in the order they entered the group. Each person was required to put in $7000 cash. The first person on the list then got $7000 from each of the next seven people, and their name was removed from the top of the list, and the next person on the list moved to the top. Then, the people on the list each tried to get as many people to join as they could, with each one putting in $7000. Once seven more people joined and each put in $7000, the person on top of the list got that money and was removed from the list. It kept going, and the top person got the money each time seven new people joined.

Often, when a person got paid, they would reinvest $7000 or more and put their name at the bottom of the list. Some even invested money on other lists to try to increase their payouts. Many tried to start their own list so they could have their name at the top and get paid right away. They usually added family members under their name on the new list. How successful they were depended on how many people they knew and how good of a salesman they were.

They got together each week at the home of the person at the top of the list so everyone could watch them get paid.

Sometimes, a few people were paid depending on how many people were convinced to join that week. It made others believe they could get their share and they worked harder to recruit others.

Watching a person or several persons receive $49,000 in cash would inspire most people to keep going at least until their name got to the top of the list.

As with most small get-rich-quick schemes, the people started fighting amongst themselves when they felt someone wasn't working hard enough to recruit others.

The closer a person's name got to the top of the list, the more they pushed others to find more people so they could get paid.

That's also when the fear and embarrassment of losing their money started growing.

Unfortunately, too many people started their own lists and they began running out of people willing to invest. Once that happened, the investors started demanding their $7000 back from the person they had given it to. Of course they were told to get lost which led to people filling complaints within their departments.

I know this because I was working for the Police department at the time and had been approached to invest money in the game. I told them no. My reasons were first that it was illegal, and second that because I knew when it finally collapsed, many people were going to lose their money. I didn't want to be one of the people responsible for that. I did know people who collected their $49,000 a couple of times and others who lost their money on more than one list.

When I told the people it was a Ponzi scheme and illegal, they claimed it wasn't because they called it by another name. I don't remember what that name was.

When it comes to get-rich-quick schemes, people can convince themselves of almost anything to justify stealing money from others.

When I told them others were going to lose their money, they said, they needed to bring in more people so they wouldn't. So much for caring about others.

Once the departmental investigations started, the departments realized that many top ranking people were involved, so the investigations were quickly closed down.

Some people were quietly told to give back some of the money, but many because of greed and fear lost everything they invested.

Some of our biggest systems, social security, and retirement and pensions plans, fail because the money is taken out for uses other than what they were intended, or they were never fully funded. That's because the companies that are supposed to be funding them used the money to make their bottom line look better. That increased their stock value so those at the top could cash out larger amounts-the same as those running the Ponzi scheme pulling out money to buy things for themselves.

Look at how many companies went out of business, and the employees found out their pensions were never fully funded, or the company had used the money to try and save the company. Sears and Kmart are great examples of this problem.

Those older pension plans were set up for the company to pay retirees until they died, and some even paid the spouse after the retiree's death.

Sears CEO blamed the retirees for Sears' failure. He said the money paid to them meant the company could only invest a little money back into the business.

In case you were wondering about Sears and Kmart retiree's, the courts are working to ensure that a part of any money made from the sales of Sears brands, goes to the retirement fund.

Many of the retirement plans today are 401k styles. That means the people are responsible for investing their retirement money, so the company isn't on the hook for pensions if it closes its doors. Does that benefit the companies or their employees?

Look at how much money unions pull from their underfunded pension plans to fund political campaigns, and other activities to get laws changed in their favor. They do this in the hope they can get more contracts, thus more workers, to increase the incoming money supply. That way, no one catches on to the fact they are a Ponzi scheme.

All these systems require more people at the bottom to contribute money than there are people at the top taking money. In the case of stores, they need to sell more goods and spend less on employees.

Retirement systems especially need more people putting money into them because more people draw money from them every year.

One plan I'm a member of made a smart decision when it was developed. They made everyone pay into the system for five years before anyone could receive a disbursement. The idea was to build a good base amount before anything was taken out.

Unfortunately, it wasn't too many years after they started paying out, that they had to cut the original amount they were going to pay a person each month and increase the amount those still paying in had to contribute.

Because they were putting in more each month, they were promised a higher monthly return when they retired then the original people were receiving. The system is still working because more people are still being hired and paying in.

At this time, I don't know how much the working members have to pay in each month. The point is that without the system being adjusted, more money being put in, it would've quickly failed.

If the retirement system gives yearly raises based on inflation, it will require even more people to contribute, an increase in the money each person has to put in, or higher returns on its investments to keep going.

Look at how much money the retirement systems lost during the Covid lockdown period. They were paying out, but little to nothing was coming in.

Most of the money from retirement systems is invested in the stock markets and we already know how unstable they are. There are times when the wealthy, big investment firms, and the government dump money into the markets to keep them artificially inflated and afloat. These so called random systems are all controlled.

It's done so the small investors, along with the retirement and pension funds, keep funding a system that allows the top people and firms to pull even more money from the system. Remember, the investment companies get paid whether anyone makes or loses money in the markets.

All retirement systems require and plan on a higher rate of return from their investments to keep functioning than the members of that plan contribute.

Experts say capitalism isn't a pyramid scheme because it produces goods and services, whereas a typical pyramid scheme produces nothing of value. I disagree with that. The pyramid scheme produces income for those who get in early. The money or income it provides allows the receivers to buy goods and services.

Without a way to purchase the goods and services, the goods and services are of no value.

A problem with capitalism is goods and services are only produced if someone can make money from them. It's called supply and demand. It doesn't matter what is needed or wanted; only what they can create a large market for.

A supply and demand system is only good for those who can afford it. I live in Las Vegas a city with over 150,000 hotel rooms and many professional sporting events and concerts. The hotel room rates and event ticket prices change daily based on how many people want them.

It's the same with airline tickets, rooms on cruise ships, and almost any event where people want a temporary distraction from everyday life or a vacation.

Is it right that one day a hotel room is $79 and the next day the same room is $300?

It's the same with food items when a study tells people something is now good for them. The odds are it was an item that wasn't selling very well and the suppliers had a lot of stock on hand.

When the study gets released saying how good it is for us, which was done by those who produced the items, the suppliers and sellers raise the price because they think people will pay it based on their propaganda-sales campaign.

I remember when we were told butter was bad for us. Butter is just one of the many foods over the years that was good for us and then bad for us and then back to good for us.

At the same time the reports butter was bad came out, there just happened to be a boat load of new margarine products hitting the stores, and commercials on television telling us how great it was for us.

Fast forward a few years and people are being told how bad margarine is for them and how good some real butter is for them.

Under a capitalist system, all markets are actually created by the producers, not the consumers. For those who have been reading my other books, you know that getting people to want or think they need certain items, is another matrix program.

This might be a good time to think about why you want the things you want and from where you got the idea that you wanted or need them. If nobody told you a new pair of shoes were now on the market, would you still believe you needed them?

The concept of capitalism is that when something is selling well or in high demand, more people will start producing it thus reducing the price over time: supply and demand.

I'll again use Las Vegas as an example. In the early 2020s when business were shut down from Covid and many people were losing their homes, they realized there was a lack of apartments for people to move-be forced into. With interest rates going up at the same time, there were even more people that couldn't afford to buy homes.

Because there weren't many apartments for them to rent, the developers and investors started going crazy building apartment buildings.

Because of the supply and demand concept, the system's desire for profit, and the time it takes to build those places, we now have a large number of unaffordable apartments with more being built.

Because of the now larger supply, eventually the rents will have to come down so more people can afford them, but in the meantime, a lot of people will not be able to afford a place to live. It's the pendulum effect. We have perceived shortages to drive up the prices, then excess to bring them back down where they should've been all along. The real problem is, the scarcities are purposely created and planned for by those at the top. They make the money when the prices go up quickly because they already have the goods available.

They cause the prices to drop, then step in and buy up what's available, which then drives up the prices so they can resell for a profit.

Does the apartment building craze in Las Vegas mean that in the near future they plan to collapse the housing market again? This time, they would already have the apartments ready for those who lose their homes.

The developers and investors started building apartments because they knew that eventually, the laws passed during Covid preventing people from being kicked out of their homes, including home rentals, would expire, and people would need a place to live.

Rather than building those apartments to help give people affordable places to live, they built them looking for future profits.

There will be some who don't accept what I'm saying about the housing and land markets being that controlled, so I'll give you a couple examples that might open your eyes.

The following is a market control plan that has been used successfully and repeatedly.

If you really looked around your area you will see evidence of what I'm going to write about.

Do you remember the news and YouTube videos showing homeless camps set up on the sidewalks in front of the beachfront businesses in southern California? There were rows of businesses and homes that had been vandalized and closed down because no customers wanted to enter that area due to the homeless camps and all the garbage and drugs they tend to leave around the area. People didn't feel safe going there. The controllers were using the underlying program of this reality to get what they wanted: **FEAR**.

Those stores and buildings were once high-rent and income areas. Once the homeless were allowed to move in, and yes, they were allowed to move in, the businesses couldn't get anyone to rent or buy their buildings for anything close to what they paid for them.

After the homeless camps have been there long enough and that problem has been covered extensively by the willing puppet media, enough to destroy the building's owners investments, investment firms will come in and buy those beach-front buildings for pennies on a dollar. It wouldn't be long after that buyout happens behind the scenes; the city will announce plans to move the homeless camps and revitalize those areas. To restore those areas to once again attract tourists and investors. Who will make the money when that happens, the new investors or those who had to sell out?

I saw the same thing happen here in Las Vegas. There was an area on North Las Vegas Blvd just North of downtown Las Vegas where it met the city of North Las Vegas. The area consisted of large vacant lots and some older run-down businesses.

At one point, the homeless were allowed to set up their camps along the sidewalk for the entire length of that area.

Of course, they spilled over onto the empty land and left piles of garbage, human waste, and old needles, just like they do in every area they're allowed to occupy for any length of time.

Once the homeless had moved in that area, they began getting media coverage along with plenty of videos on YouTube showing all the problems with that area.

One day, we drove by that area to see the mess it had become. There were tents and thrown-together shelters all along the sidewalk and land, just as had been shown.

I told Irina that letting the homeless camp there was part of a plan to lower the land values so that investors could come in and buy the entire area for pennies on a dollar.

The city was allowing the homeless to camp there because behind the scenes, either knowing or unknowingly, they were working with the developers.

I said that at some point that land will be sold and the entire area developed as part of a revitalization effort. When that happens, the homeless would quietly be moved to the next area the investors want to drop the value of.

A few months later, we drove by that area and saw that all the homeless were gone, and a portable chain-link fence had been placed along the sidewalk all around the land.

On the land, sat some construction equipment showing they were getting ready to develop it. I don't remember the story of the homeless getting moved out ever making the local news.

Every part of the economy is controlled by a matrix program.

Pharmaceutical companies are another example of capitalism at its best. They only work on developing a new medicine if there will be enough demand to recoup the money they claim they invested in research and production, and to make a shit load more beyond that investment.

Remember how I said the media helps the controllers to influence the public and create fear of whatever they want? Problem, reaction, solution. Are the diseases they claim are killing mass amounts of people really doing it? Why do you automatically believe whatever numbers the news and government give you, especially when they call it a crisis?

They have pushed high cholesterol as being the cause behind the rise in heart disease. Once the public became afraid of high cholesterol, I saw a story on the local news that suggested a cholesterol lowering drug should be added to every towns water supply to help cut down on heart disease.

As far as I know, that idea wasn't adopted by any city and it was never put on the news again.. Who would've benefited from providing all the medicines needed to do that across the entire U.S? Can you imagine the side effects it would've caused in millions of people unknowingly taking that drug?

How many more medical visits would it have generated when people started having problems without knowing why?

What if they saw that the majority of people had certain results in their blood tests when they got to certain ages and decided to create a fear based campaign saying anyone with those blood test results will eventually get a certain disease. That the only chance a person has to prevent that disease or at least lessen it, is to take this new medicine. Just an idea to think about.

It doesn't matter how serious a disease is or how much those with it suffer; unless the company can sell a shit load of that drug, they don't even work on it. In 2022 the pharmaceutical companies worldwide, made approx. $1.48 trillion dollars U.S.

When they do produce a drug because of political or public pressure that can help a smaller number of people, the prices are so high that no one without insurance can afford it.

Even then, because insurance companies are all about the bottom line, most would refuse to cover the cost of such an expensive drug. They don't want to take money out of their investors pockets just to help someone get better. A sick population equals more income and more investors.

They also don't work on medicines that would cure most major illnesses because they can only cure a person once, but they can treat their symptoms every month for a lifetime.

Our entire medical system is set up the same way: treat the symptoms and/or make a person worse because of the treatment or medicine, and you'll have a patient/income for life.

When doctors or dentist retire and sell their practices, they are selling their customer base because it's the only product they produce.

Capitalism does provide us with plenty of items in our stores and a great variety of choices of the same thing in different wrappers. Do we really need 20 different toothpastes? Why not just one that works?

Those who support capitalism say that people in capitalist economies have strong incentives to work hard, increase efficiency, and produce superior products. By rewarding ingenuity and innovation, the market maximizes economic growth and individual prosperity while providing a variety of goods and services for consumers.

By encouraging the production of desirable goods and services and discouraging the production of unwanted or unnecessary ones, the marketplace self-regulates, leaving less room for government interference and mismanagement.

But, capitalism does not guarantee that each person's basic needs will be met. That's because market mechanisms are mechanical rather than normative and agnostic concerning social effects.

The idea that capitalism encourages people to produce superior products is incorrect. Look at how many items China sells worldwide because they can make a lower quality product at a cheaper price. Look at the growth of sellers like Harbor Freight and Temu.

Go to any store, and you'll see different product quality levels. The best version, which lasts the longest and is most efficient, is always priced so high that only a handful of people can afford to buy them.

Everyone else is forced to settle for a lower-quality item, that is guaranteed to wear out or break down, ensuring that people have to buy another one down the road. Capitalism encourages providing items or services that guarantee the customers will have to return for another product or service. That's why electronic products each have their own type of plug or charging device.

Just like the medical field, the products treat symptoms because the focus is always on the bottom line and returning customers!

There are many problems with capitalism as it's practiced in the United States and many other countries, even though most people like and support the idea of capitalism. They want to keep the system in place because they're still hoping to get their piece of the pie.

Capitalism, by its design, creates a vast wealth gap, with those at the top getting more and more over time while the value of what those at the lower levels have keeps getting smaller.

Most people don't realize that their jobs, no matter how much they get paid, always produce more money for the owner than he pays the employees doing the work.

That's why credit is readily given, and debt is encouraged for the working class. It forces people to keep working and providing income for those at the top.

Have you heard the old saying, "I sold my soul to the company store?" It's about the old mining days when most mines were in remote areas. Since there weren't cars or freeways for the workers to commute on, the mines built housing, which the workers rented, and a small town to provide services where the workers often lived with their families. The only place for the workers to get food and supplies was at a store owned and run by the mining company, the company store.

These stores gave new workers credit for rent and supplies against their future wages. Because they had a monopoly on everything, the stores charged much higher prices for goods and services. Wages were low, so it was only a short time before the workers owed the mining company more than they were getting paid. Thus, the workers worked in the mines for what amounted to free. The mines had people to watch the workers to make sure they didn't try and leave without paying what they owed.

Has anything really changed since those days?

Because of cars and freeways, we no longer have to live where we work or buy supplies from just one store. We can live anywhere we can afford, as long as we're willing to drive back and forth, and shop at whatever store seems to be cheapest.

With prices-expenses always going up, the cost of health care, day-care, having to pay income, property, sales, and state taxes on whatever we earn, the only thing that's actually changed is we no longer have to live where we work: that is if we can afford the expense of computing. Let's call it living in a bigger box, but it's still a box owned by the companies.

It's still the company that builds and sells us the homes, runs the stores, and even sells us the cars that we think gives us some freedom. If you think you actually own the home you live in, try not paying the property tax and see how long it is before the company takes it back from you. Don't register-pay the yearly taxes on your car, and see how long you're allowed to drive on the roads built by your tax dollars.

The company still hires people to enforce their rules, law enforcement, courts, tax collectors, and collection agencies, and ensure no one gets away without paying. How long can you drive your car to work if you can't afford the gas or the cost of repairs?

Everything you produce at work still belongs to your employer, the same as the farmers living under Feudalism. You still get taxed by the King, the federal government, and the Nobles, your state and local governments. Who do you think you're paying your property and sales tax to?

Entering the Fourth Dimensional Matrix

As I said before, even if you think you own your home and have a piece of paper that says it's yours, stop paying the local Noble the taxes he changes for allowing you to live there, and he'll take his house back. Not only that, but he expects you to pay for the upkeep of his property.

You can move to another area or state, but you still end up living under the thumb of the local Noble.

Every inch of land is still claimed by some government entity same as the days of Feudalism.

In the old days, you couldn't hunt on the King's land. Now, you can hunt on the King's land, but he requires you to pay for a permit, tells you when you can do it, and how much you can take from his land. It's the same with trees for lumber or firewood. He even has officers to check and ensure you're following his rules, just like the Knights of old.

You could refuse to work and see if you qualify for welfare and free housing. Before you do, you might want to look at where that free housing is located and what it looks like.

You could live like the homeless on the streets or under bridges, but you'll only be allowed to live there until they need you to move someplace else and lower the property values.

If you've watched the news over the last year, you'll notice they are allowing the homeless to live on the sidewalks and set up camps in many wealthy and business areas of San Francisco. However this is not the case in areas where the nobles or their minions live. After reading what I wrote about why the homeless are allowed to live in certain places for a time, you'll understand what the goal is in San Francisco and any other place where you hear about the local government allowing the homeless to set up camps.

I'm adding this paragraph in April 2024 to show some evidence of what I had written about above.

I saw a recent headline about some condos in San Francisco that are located not far from the Tenderloin district in San Francisco. The Tenderloin area is one of the areas where they have been having a lot of problems with the homeless and crime.

April 16, 2024. A condominium in downtown San Francisco, an area that's been rocked by several problems in the past few years, was sold last week for about half of its purchase price in 2019, as shown on real estate marketplace Zillow.

The property, a two-bedroom, two-bathroom condo on 1075 Market St, a five-minute driving distance from Union Square and a three-minute driving distance from the troubled neighborhood of Tenderloin, was listed for sale on Zillow on January 18 for $695,000.

After spending months on the market, it was sold on April 8 for $675,000 — about half of the price commanded by the condo in late May 2019, when it was sold for $1,250,000.

Most other housing markets and areas are still going up in price. Once investors buy up enough of the homes that are selling for .50 cents on a dollar and they then clean out the homeless in San Francisco, those places will go up in value.

Many people in our society are living check to check. Some because they just don't make much money, and others because of the large debt they've accumulated trying to buy everything they're told they should have and feel they deserve.

Just like at the company store, they're given whatever they want and told not to worry about it; that it will be taken out of their wages later on. That's the same mentality the federal government has when it comes to spending.

If you've read my other books, you know about this reality being one of wanting, desire, and never being satisfied no matter what we get.

Once we get something we want, we're already looking for the next thing we want. It's an ego-driven reality.

There is no genuine concern from those who have to help provide for those who do the work for them. So much food is wasted, plowed under, or not grown because there isn't enough money to be made by growing or sharing it. Look at all the buildings and homes sitting empty while many are forced to live in their cars or on the street. There is more than enough of everything on this world to ensure everyone has a good standard of living, but capitalism isn't designed to provide for or care about that.

At times, the government attempts to step in, socialism, and get those at the top to provide more for those below. At the same time, they don't want to piss off those at the top, because without their campaign donations, the politicians don't get to stay in office and live their comfortable protected lives.

There was a time under capitalism when the average person could save enough money from working to buy a house or go to college without incurring large amounts of debt. Nowadays, look at how many people have large student debt and an even larger mortgage.

Throw in a car payment and every other expense we now have, and you'll realize that under capitalism we have moved backward in what our wages will buy us rather than forward. It used to be a college degree guaranteed a person a job, now less than half will get a job in the field their degree is in.

As you can see by what I wrote, capitalism has just given us the illusion of freedom and choice over feudalism.

We have the same illusion in every area of this 3D matrix. As I mentioned, it's a bigger box, but none the less, still a box.

I cover much more detail on the illusion of choice and free will in my first book, Truth Beyond the Earthly Matrix, and would refer you there for more details.

I think I beat up capitalism enough, so let's move on to socialism.

Socialism

Ha-Joon Chang in his book, 23 things they don't tell you about capitalism wrote: "Contrary to what is commonly believed, the performance of developing countries in a period of state led development was superior to what they have achieved during the subsequent period of market-oriented reform.

There were some spectacular failures of state intervention, but most of these countries grew much faster, with more equitable income distribution and far fewer economic crisis, during the 'bad old days' than they have done in the period of market oriented reforms. Moreover, it is also not true that almost all rich countries have become rich through free market policies. The truth is more or less the opposite.

With only a few exceptions, all of today's rich countries, including Britain and the U.S.-the supposed homes of free trade and free market-have become rich through the combination of protectionism, subsidies and other policies that today they advise developing countries not to adopt. Free market have made few countries rich so far and will make few rich in the future." End.

What is socialism? Socialism is where the means of production, factories, farms, offices, basically the things that produce for the economy, are held by all in common and subject to democratic decision making rather than by a few individuals.

This doesn't necessarily mean it's run by the government but in socialist countries like Cuba and Venezuela, the government owns and runs almost everything.

By definition of the word, there are no pure socialist countries. Those countries that are called socialist by the world, are usually a combination of systems. They range from tightly controlled dictatorships like North Korea and Cuba, to more socialist-capitalist countries like Finland and Sweden.

Countries like, China, Cuba, Lao Peoples Democratic Republic, the Socialist Republic of Vietnam, and Russia are considered Marxist-Leninist states.

The new government, led by Vladimir Lenin, established the Russian Soviet Federative Socialist Republic (RSFSR), the world's first constitutionally socialist state.

In 1972, Juche replaced Marxism–Leninism in the revised North Korean constitution as the official state ideology, this being a response to the Sino-Soviet split. Juche was nonetheless defined as a creative application of Marxism-Leninism.

Venezuela considered itself a socialist country since its run by the far left socialist party.

As defined by Wikipedia socialism means; Socialism is an economic and political philosophy encompassing diverse economic and social systems characterized by social ownership of the means of production, as opposed to private ownership.

Socialism as a political tradition emerged as a reaction against the industrial revolution. It was also an offshoot of and against liberalism

Socialists want freedom for everyone. They believe everyone has the right to education, food, health care, a decent place to live, to be part of a democratic body, and to have enough free and leisure time to pursue things like art and music; to do things they enjoy.

Within a capitalistic system, a lack of money keeps many people from enjoying these rights. It's often asked by socialists, how many Michelangelo, Leonardo da Vinci, or Einstein's were never allowed to contribute to the world because they didn't have the money to pursue formal training or education, get noticed by their chosen field, and develop their inventions.

Within the workplace instead focusing just on the bottom line, how much profit can be gained, and how much more work can be gotten from the workers without paying them more, socialists want to look at incentives that can benefit everyone. It allows for central planning and free association between cooperatives. Everyone should be allowed input before changes in how things are done are made.

With our current system, a single person or a small group makes all the decisions about changes in how things are done. They do it from the viewpoint of how those changes will bring those at the top or the share holders the most money. Thoughts of how those changes might affect the workers have very little impact on those decisions.

Socialism is considered an evil word and system by most capitalists. The media puts out stories intended to vilify anyone who wants to enact socialist beliefs.

That was the label they hung around the neck of former presidential candidate Bernie Sanders. During speeches, people like former President Trump have made the idea of socialism seem akin to communism.

In truth, socialism is considered the necessary step between capitalism and communism.

A socialist society rewards those who show effort and those with innovation. People can own property, but industrial production and the means of producing wealth are owned communally and managed by a democratically elected government. The people do vote in a socialist society to make changes in their society.

One criticism of socialism is that in any society where everyone holds equal wealth, there can be no material incentive to work because one does not receive rewards for a work well done. They further argue that incentives increase productivity for all people and that the loss of those effects would lead to stagnation.

Others have said the biggest problem with socialism is eventually, you run out of other people's money. That's a problem in any monetary system.

Communism

A pure communist society, according to Marx, is a political, economic, and social system in which most or all property and resources are collectively owned by a class-free society rather than by individual citizens. It creates a society where all people are equal, and there is no need for money or the accumulation of individual wealth. The central government controls all facets of production.

Production output is distributed according to the needs of the people. The central government provides basic necessities such as food, housing, medical care, and education. This allows everyone to share equally the results of the collective labor. There is no private property in a communist society. Something like the hippy communities of the 60s where everyone worked and shared everything.

There are currently no pure communist countries in the world today.

The ideas and practice of communism and socialism grew out of the industrial revolution, during which management had control and took advantage of the workers.

It's when the unions started organizing the workers. If you watch some of the old movies, you'll see the use of strikebreakers during that time.

They were groups of thugs hired by the owners to inflict or instill the fear of physical harm if the workers didn't go back to work and forget about joining a union.

Both systems look to the government or collective organizations rather than individuals to run and control production.

Within communism, the central government is responsible for all economic planning relating to supply and demand.

Many people still believe the governments of what were and still are socialistic societies were communist.

I remember as a kid in school during the 1960s and 1970s, being told to fear communist Russia. They wanted to take over the world and take away everything we had. If we didn't fight them, we'd be standing in bread lines just like them.

I didn't know it at the time, but they were actually socialists, not communists.

It was even in the name of the county. U.S.S.R., Union of Soviet Socialist Republics, but the media and government kept using the word communists to brainwash us.

Here are some benefits and problems with the old Soviet socialist system.

I had the chance to visit the cities of Kiev and Odessa in the Ukraine in 1993, which is two years after the official flag of Russia came down.

The people I spent a week with were very open about how they felt about the fall of what I thought at the time was communism, and the rise of capitalism in their country.

They preferred the old system because they knew they would have food, free higher education based on a person's ability, medical care, and a place to live. A lady gave me an example of why they liked it better than the developing capitalism system.

When she was in college, everyone received money to buy food and they didn't have to worry about working. College was also free, so they could focus on learning and were given a job after graduating.

She said her nephew, who was now in college, didn't receive any money from the government and had to live on potatoes because he couldn't afford to buy anything else.

The rent in her apartment had gone from nothing to over 1/3 of her monthly salary of $15.00 U.S.

Because of capitalism, the value of their currency and food prices changed daily. During my time there, one U.S dollar went from being worth 3,000 coupons-their dollar was called a coupon at that time-to over 8,000 coupons per dollar when I left.

That's why they converted their money to U.S. dollars as soon as they received their pay.

To get a better exchange rate on my U.S. money, we traded dollars on the street with currency dealers. It was illegal at the time, so we had to be careful when doing it.

My hotel room was $60. U.S. a night. Compared to her apartment rent, that was a crazy price.

At that time people visiting the Ukraine were required to stay in certain hotels. There was also a different pricing system for their citizens and for foreign visitors. Whenever we went somewhere, they always paid because it was a lot cheaper.

I always paid them back in U.S. dollars so they made money.

When I brought something at a store the exchange rate was great for me because everyone wanted U.S. dollars. I remember buying an entire pie for what would've been .25 cents U.S.

During my time there, we took an overnight train ride from Kiev to Odessa and back the next night. Tickets for a sleeping car cost about $15 per person for the round trip.

That may sound great, except that it only included the room. Bedding was extra, there was no water in the room or on the train, and no food or drinks were served on the train. The bathrooms, which only had toilets, no showers or sinks, were in another part of the train. The toilet had no seat to sit on or toilet paper, and when you lifted the top lid and looked down, you saw the train tracks going by.

Yeah, there was no holding tank, so everything landed on the tracks as the train sped by.

Another problem that hit the people of the former Russian socialist countries when the wall come down, was the ruble and other currencies were now allowed to be greatly affected by the dollar. People who had retired under the old system found that their retirement money no longer provided for them. Their dollar value went down while prices went up. They received no increase in their retirement to cover the difference so many had to return to work.

My wife talked with some of them at the airport in Moscow who were forced to sell toilet paper to people in the airports bathrooms so they could afford food and rent. Every public bathroom I went in, including the airports, had no toilet seats, toilet paper, or anything to wipe your hands on after washing.

My wife grew up under the old Soviet system, in Kazakhstan, and there were many things she liked about it. Most of the benefits are similar to those of other current socialist systems, except they were much cheaper then.

Everyone had a job, an income, free medical care, and a place to live. Higher education was free. What job or school the kids went to depended on testing, how well they did in school, and their grades.

Everyone according to their ability. The better students got the better choices regarding what college/institute they went to and what jobs they received.

That may sound great, except a student's grades could be improved if the parents had money or were in higher positions.

Because most working people didn't receive much money, they were always open to taking bribes. Bribes are pretty much standard practice in third world countries. In this country, we call them tips, commissions, and bonuses.

Those bribes could include hard to get food items instead of money because other than the basic foods, they didn't have much available. If the person needing something had some influence, they could promise someone a promotion to a better paying job, and for the poorer female students, having sex with the teacher or boss also worked.

As terrible as it may now sound to us, sex was often required from the prettier females for job promotions and to get out of any trouble they might have gotten in. The same thing used to happen in our country so we shouldn't be surprised that it happened in poorer countries.

The same thing still happens in the U.S. education system. Remember the parents on trial for paying over $500,000 in bribes, donations, so their daughter could get into a better school?

Even though their medical care wasn't top of the line it was free, and that included hospital stays. When a woman had a baby she received up to two years off work with pay, and in some cases, five years off work with pay.

If you weren't feeling well and didn't want to go to work, you called the ambulance. They, along with a doctor, came to your home and gave you an excuse to stay home for up to a week.

Medicines were free, and you could get a prescription or tell the pharmacist what was wrong and they gave you want you needed. That included some pain meds like codeine.

There were also a lot of problems associated with this type of socialist society.

There were always shortages of certain foods, especially if they had to be imported. Bread and vodka were always in the stores since the prices and supplies were controlled by the government. Some items like sugar were controlled by vouchers given to each person. Again, you could get more if you knew someone or gave the person issuing the vouchers a nice gift.

The kids under 16 had to work on collective farms in the summer. My wife said you got a shower once a week, and the hours were long and hard when it came to working the fields. She said she worked in the kitchen and had to be there at 4AM.

It was hit and miss in the stores with what we would call everyday items.

If you knew someone at the store or had political connections, you had a better chance of getting what you wanted. When deliveries or new items came into the store many were sold out the back door to friends and family, and what was left was put on the store shelves for others to buy.

It was well known that those of high rank in the military or good positions in the government had their own stores, hospitals, housing, and vacation homes.

Everyone stole or took bribes no matter what job or position they held because it was the only way they could improve their lives.

There was always a shortage of good winter clothing and the shoes were of terrible quality. They were imported from China and often had no insoles and very little support.

When they got wet in the winter, they didn't last very long. When I went to the Ukraine, I asked what I could bring for them. They said shoes. Even into the late 90s whenever Irina went to visit her family, she always took a suitcase of good quality shoes to give to her family and sell to others.

Housing was given based on the size of the family and the rank or political status of the person. After the collapse of the Russian states, people could submit paperwork to get ownership of the apartment or home they were living in.

Most of the housing, especially the apartments, were built after world War 2 and made of cement. Water and, especially hot water in the apartments, was controlled and limited. It was the same with heating. You didn't take showers nor did you change clothes every day because most people didn't have washing machines and no one had dryers.

They had to air dry clothes on racks in the homes, which led to humidity and a smelly apartment.

There was often no toilet paper so they used rags which then had to be washed. There was no deodorant. The same held true for female sanitary products.

They used mainly radiators for heat. Some homes had wood stoves but not in the apartment buildings. The heat was turned on in the fall on a certain date and off in the spring on a certain date. It didn't matter what the weather was outside.

The water came on and off randomly, and was costly, so they had to gather what they could during the times it was on.

They usually brought food at outdoor green markets because the stores had very little. They bought whatever the farmers had, including meat, mostly lamb. There were no refrigerators at the outdoor markets.

I remember watching a lady selling fish that were laying on old newspapers on the ground.

Sitting behind them she spent her time with a fan, trying to keep the flies off. Most of the time, she failed miserly.

There was no prepackaged food, so everyone had to cook their meals. I will say the food was fresh and tasted good. Whenever you visited someone they fed you even if they didn't have much. Those with more money of course served better meals to impress their guests.

I guess things are the same no matter what country you live in.

There were no homeless people living on the streets during the Russian times because everyone had a place to live. The harder a person's job was physically the more they got paid.

Construction people and miners got paid more than the doctors because their jobs took a greater and faster toll on the body.

There were people who didn't want to work and they did have a harder life, but that was their choice.

When the wall came down and the Russian countries were starting with capitalism, the mentality of the workers when it came to working, caused many problems when outside companies came in and started investing in those places.

When I was in the Ukraine, I talked with some German business men who had brought into some of the business in Kiev. They said they had come over there because much of the money, over one million dollars, and most the products that had been sent over, had disappeared.

The products were being sold out the back door like the workers were used to doing and they'd kept the money.

The money sent to build up the business had been used by the business owners to get things they wanted rather than to help build the business.

They said many of the workers only showed up when they wanted to because under the old Soviet system nobody did more than what was required and took time off whenever they wanted.

He said it was very frustrating for foreign investors who were used to people working.

It was hard for people to change from a socialism mindset where you always had a job and no one expected much from you, to one of capitalism where you either worked for yourself or for others who expected you to work so they could make a profit.

Other current socialist countries operate differently. Those like North Korea and Cuba are tightly controlled by the government. If what we hear or read about the status of the people is correct, most are suffering because of a lack of many everyday items in their daily lives.

China has allowed more private business ownership and outside companies to set up business, so overall the people are better off financially than in North Korea and Cuba.

The Scandinavian countries are socialist/capitalist, yet are better balanced when it comes to business ownership and what their people have. They have free higher education and free medical, as well as other programs that help the people. Overall the average person is better off and happier in those countries than in other countries. They consistently rank among the highest in polls for overall life happiness.

There are more billionaires per capita in Sweden, Finland, and Denmark than in the United States. This is in spite of being more heavily taxed and paying for most of the services given to other citizens of their countries. It sounds like the idea of we'll let you get rich as long as you provide money/services for those who have less.

The average person there is more willing to open a business and take a chance on their idea than in the United States.

With free medical care and a basic income, they know that if their business fails, they will still be able to have a decent life.

This encourages people to develop their ideas and take a chance on success even knowing they'll be paying a lot of income taxes if they succeed.

In the U.S., if a person tries to develop their idea or open a business and it fails, they often end up broke and in debt, with little to no income. Most aren't willing to take that chance, so many good ideas die before getting off the ground.

Another problem with socialism is, as I mentioned earlier, eventually, you run out of other people's money.

Like all Ponzi schemes, you'll always need more money coming in as the number of people getting the money increases and the cost of those services goes up.

There is currently an experimental program in California where a group of people are given a basic income each month. They can spend it on whatever they want.

Those studying the experiment have noticed that the people receiving the money have been spending it on everyday household expenses, such as rent, food, and insurance.

This type of program can only exist if taxes are raised on those who are working and the large companies, like a socialist system, or the government takes over ownership of everything, much like a communist system, so all the money made goes to them. From there it can be handed out to those that need it.

This experiment was started partly because of the development of AI and people like Elon Musk stating that as time goes on, there will be less jobs for people.

With robotics and AI rapidly expanding, much of the production and distribution processes will be taken over.

You're seeing the first signs of that now with the huge Amazon warehouses and packages being delivered by drones and self-driving cars.

Fast food places are slowly getting rid of their employees by allowing people to order from their phones and from kiosks in the stores.

Another new development I wanted to add here as evidence what I'm writing is happening. In California the new min. wage is now $20 an hour.

Many fast food and small business are saying paying that wage will drive them out of business. Less small business mean more business for the larger companies.

The last thing most businesses want to do is share the money their employees are making for them with the employees.

These business owners have to make some decisions. They can raise their prices and see if people will still pay the higher price for their goods and services. It might mean they would have to improve the quality of their products to keep people interested.

Of course that might mean their costs would go up in order to use better quality items.

If possible within their business, they can look at bringing in technology to replace as many workers as possible. Remember I mentioned earlier that would be the next step in businesses trying to cut down on the amount of workers needed. Having people get used to ordering food online or from kiosks was the first step in that process.

The franchises, big companies, will have the best chance at bringing in the tech. because their parent companies will be able to foot the bill, then charge it back to the owners, giving them the advantage over privately owned businesses.

The rich will get richer.

This is another step in forcing changes on people to prepare them for the future. Companies will tell customers that in order to keep food prices at a level people can afford, they need to bring in robots. People wanting the lowest prices will quickly agree to this step.

It wouldn't be long before robots are preparing and serving the food.

You already saw some restaurants bring in robots to deliver food to the tables when they couldn't hire enough people. There are many large stores with self guided floor cleaning machines.

Most grocery stores and businesses now have their own delivery or pickup services. Several companies and people make a good living delivering takeout foods and other items to a person's home.

It's a shift in the types of jobs people can do and a transition to a point where items will be delivered by robots of some kind.

Each step makes the next one and the ultimate goal easier for people to accept.

I buy many items on line from places like Amazon and Walmart that offer next day or the same day delivery. It saves me driving, parking, and walking around the stores with all the people. I just have to be willing to wait a day or two for the items. Over time that delivery time will drop even more. Right now I still have the option to go to a store and get what I want. Eventually that option will go away.

Many chain stores are going with self checkout lines, so they've cut down on the number of employees needed.

At some point the checkout scanners will be able to scan all the items in the cart without them having to be removed.

They'll use magnetic or electronic UPC codes on all items. Much like they do now for expensive items that have a tag inside. Currently the tag gets disabled when the item is scanned.

After that, instead of picking up the items you want from the shelves, you'll select or scan them from a display and they will be waiting for you at the checkout, already paid for.

No more stealing, so more money for the companies. Do you think they'll pass on that savings to us as lower prices?

It won't be long before robots will be stocking the store shelves. Eventually, the inside of stores will change, so the shelves we now see with items stocked, will be gone. It could end up just being a bunch of kiosks like at the fast food places where you'll place your order and they'll be delivered to you.

You will order what you want, and a robot will get the item for you from the warehouse. There'll be no need to even enter the business.

Add in electronic currency paid online and drones delivering the items, and we wouldn't have to even leave the house.

Much of this became acceptable as a result of the Covid lockdown. I wouldn't be surprised if, in the big picture, that was one of the reasons for the extended Covid lockdown time. It forced businesses to develop ways to get their products to the consumers without the consumers leaving home or entering their businesses. Of course, the bigger companies already had the resources in place to deal with that problem. This may be why their wealth increased by $1.5 trillion during Covid.

Since people were told to be afraid of Covid, this made the desired transition even more acceptable.

Remember the favorite tactic of governments and large businesses I mentioned earlier? "Problem, reaction, solution." They create a problem, escalate fear, and then offer a solution. The solution is what they wanted to do in the first place, but they knew people would fight it if they presented it directly.

Covid and all the changes it caused fit well within this problem, reaction, and solution format.

The major expense of most companies are employee wages and benefits. Get rid of the employees, except maybe IT guys, and the companies will make a lot more money. Add in AI running the computers, and the IT guys will be out of work as well.

By giving people a basic living monthly income, they'll still be able to buy the products being produced, and the manufacturers will make even more money. Remember the monthly income, aka unemployment, many received during the Covid lockdown? It's another part of the training process.

Add in electronic currency with no cash transactions, and robots will easily be able to handle the checkout at most businesses, especially if it was already paid before the customer showed up.

After reading the last couple of pages, you might be asking why I went into more depth than you thought I would on capitalism and socialism. I wanted to point out some of the benefits and problems with each system and why they need to change. At the same time, I want you to see that those changes are already starting. Changes that, at this point in time, you might not connect to a one-world government and one world currency.

I want you to think big picture and take what seems to be unrelated events, and see how they fit together forming the foundation for a new-world.

A new 4D governmental system and a new type of economy will encompass aspects of capitalism and socialism at first. People's basic needs will have to be met and for awhile people will still feel the need to have more and benefit from their work.

The problem with any new system set up by those running the old system, is that they will always want to make sure they benefit the most. They'll want to keep their power and money, and all the material things they've accumulated.

That's the reason I feel the new 4D system, in order to be successful, at some point, will have to be set up by beings from outside our current world system. Or by those pretending to be from outside our system. AI could help set it up, but AI might not have the power to force that change, at least not at first.

It's going to require someone or a group with the power and ability to make that happen worldwide. They'll need to change the mindset of the people on Earth from one of a desire for accumulation of material things, to one of only taking what they need. People will need to see the world as a place of abundance rather than one of scarcity. That needs to happen so people won't feel the need to hoard or accumulate things.

Dividing the resources of the world for everyone rather than having them controlled by a few, and eliminating the need to limit what is produced only so money can be made, will show the world to be one of plenty rather than scarcity.

It's people that will have to change in order for any new system to work. People will change when their fears of a lack of are addressed and they see the corruption of our current systems exposed and changed.

That fear of not having in what we call the future is partially addressed within the socialist system of the Scandinavian countries. By providing free health care and a monthly living income, they have removed those fears from the minds of the people.

The elderly are also taken care of, easing the fears of many as they age of not having enough to live on.

As I mentioned, people fear the future, which is what fear is.

Nowadays, people worry about not having enough money for their retirement, not being able to buy the food they want, not being able to live in a nice home in a good area, good schools for their children, not having complete medical and dental care, not having the money to replace items like a water heater or AC unit, getting sued or ripped off, not having a job they like, and not having a job or income to live on.

The new government and monetary systems will address those issues. It will become more of a communist-type system, with everyone getting according to their needs and doing what they can according to their ability. Bringing in worldwide spirituality will help change the mindset of people.

When people don't have to worry about their future, they can relax and begin to grow spiritually. People will only be willing to share with others, rather than hoarding, when they don't view the future with fear.

If you know when you retire that, you'll be able to do the things you enjoy, have an income, or be able to go to the store and get what you need when you need it, that your medical bills are taken care of, and your children will have an equally nice future, you can relax as you age. That, in turn, will help your health.

Those of us who have spiritual knowledge, what's referred to as being awakened, already understand that idea and don't have those same worries-fears as most people.

The new world government will want a new currency or form of credit-debit so no country can complain their money wasn't used.

I wouldn't be surprised if whatever monetary system or form of asset exchange the aliens are using is one that is adopted here. It would eventually allow for interplanetary trade.

Currently, the move is towards a crypto type monetary system for each county, which over time, will merge into one system.

The goal would be to eventually be accepted into whatever Federation or conglomeration of planets the aliens belong to. Already having their system of exchange-credit in place would make sense.

Some might ask what will happen to the debt of countries if a one-world currency is adopted. The world, as we know it, has more debt than can ever be paid back. Remember, as well, that all that money was made up or created from nothing.

Here are some numbers to give you an idea of how much is owed by the world and how much is listed as assets. These numbers are available on the internet for anyone who wants to look.

I'm not going to quote all the sources for each set of numbers, because there are many sites with this information and the numbers on each are very similar.

As of 2023, the worlds debt stands at $313 trillion. That amount includes the on the books money owed by corporations, governments, and individuals. It comes out to about $40,000 for every person on the planet. It's estimated there is also another $65 trillion in hidden debt that's called, "off balance" that doesn't get talked about.

As of 2022, it's estimated that the value of all the real estate on Earth is $379.7 trillion.

That amount would vary greatly depending on how the real estate market is doing. In reality that amount means nothing unless someone is willing to buy.

As I've mentioned, the housing and land market is another game played to get the King and Nobles more money that doesn't exist. They let you live on their land, then charge you taxes for the right to live there.

If the price of the home and/or land goes up, even if it's because of improvements you have made or because of inflation, the tax collector who works for the Noble gets to take even more money from you each year. They let you improve or upgrade the home they own as long as you pay for it, and then they charge you more to live there.

Many states, counties, and cities charge a tax or fee when you sell your home. All the people you pay to sell your home, real estate, advertisers, title companies, inspectors, and more also have to claim that money as income and pay one of those nobles' taxes.

The GDP, Gross Domestic Product for the world in 2023, was $105 trillion. The world's open debt is three times more than the world produces in an entire year.

In 2022, global bank assets totaled $183 trillion. Remember that money is supposed to belong to the depositors and investors, but the banks claim it as theirs. Do you still think it's your money once you deposit it?

The global stock markets are worth approximately $109 trillion. As of 2022, the total assets of all financial institution worldwide are approximately $461.2 trillion.

The value of all gold circulating in the world is just under $10 trillion, and the market value of silver is approximately $1.788 trillion.

The problem with all these numbers is that they are interrelated and overlap, so there is no way of knowing the bottom line unless you do a lot of research. Even then, I don't think an average person would have access to enough resources to get a real answer.

The listed assets of the financial institutions, also include money owed to them, be it car loans, personal loans, home loans, or any other type of loan or investment.

The banks, in turn, have borrowed much of that money from the Federal Reserve or world banks because they have over-invested or lost the money from their depositors' and investors. In turn, the federal reserve borrows money from those banks by selling T-bills and bonds.

Banks are required to maintain a 10% reserve of depositors money. That means they can invest or spend 90% of all the deposits or money invested in their firm in any way they want.

They use your money to make money for the bank, the federal Reserve, and the federal government and pay you pennies in return.

Supposedly the federal reserve doesn't keep any profit after paying all their bills. They send any extra money made from their investments to the U.S. treasury.

The financial intuitions show what they have as an asset, but in reality, the money isn't theirs. Yet, in a way, it is because if the bank loses or spends all your money, you only get back $250,000 from the Federal government, FCID.

If another bank buys your bank, usually with a loan from the Federal Reserve, you may get your money back.

In the United States alone, the federal government has $34 trillion in debt that we're told about. The people have another $17 trillion of debt, for a total of $51 trillion.

This number doesn't count corporation debt. There is approximately $20 trillion in circulation, printed money.

That means at least $31 trillion only exist in the electronic world and have no printed money backing. It's made-up money. As of May 15, 2024, the federal reserve balance sheet, Fed's H.4.1 statement, shows a balance of $7,355,271,000,000, a little over $7.3 trillion. It's posted weekly, and anyone can look it up online.

According to Quora, approximately 8% of the worlds money supply has been printed, leaving 92% as digital money.

An example of this made-up money is as follows: You put $1000 cash in your account, which means, in theory, you can get that $1000 any time you want.

The bank you deposited it in can loan $900 of your money to someone else. Remember that they only have to have 10% of your money on hand or deposited somewhere; the other 90% they can invest for themselves. That 90% is loaned in the form of made-up electronic money, not cash.

Say they buy a T-bill from the Federal Reserve with that $900 so they can make interest from it. The Federal Reserve then loans that $900 to the federal government. That $900 is then paid to a person as social security. That person puts the $900 in their bank, believing they now have $900 they can get at any time.

Their bank, in turn, loans out or invests 90% of that money, $810, to someone else.

Your original $1000 has now become $2710, of which $1710 is made-up and never really existed. The loaning of your original $1000 continues until there's nothing left.

That's where the $31 trillion of electronic money debt came from.

What all this means is that the monetary systems of the world are all incredibly huge Ponzi schemes with money being moved around all the time, so no one realizes there isn't any money. The market crash in 2008 showed you how the system was being propped up. Like any other time the markets have crashed, it was allowed to happen for a reason. In this case, after the crash, large investors with tons of electronic money were now able to buy homes and stocks for pennies on the dollar while a lot of normal people lost their homes and investments.

Because most of the money doesn't actually exist, if there is a run on the banks or investment firms where too many people want their money, they close down and/or limit what a person can get. The same is true with companies listed on the stock market. If a large enough percentage of the people owning stocks want to cash out, the cash isn't there to pay them.

Remember earlier who, I said, owns most of the stock markets?

When we move to a one-world currency, the government debts of all countries could be forgiven by whomever takes over the new system. That would give the countries an incentive to adopt the new program.

Remember, most of that money is already electronic, so having AI take it over would be easy.

In the beginning, I don't think everyone's debt would be forgiven because that would mean all the financial intuitions would be out of business overnight.

I wouldn't rule out that as a way to get people on board with the new one-world systems, debt forgiveness could be held out as a carrot. It's the same as the current federal government forgiving-paying student loan debt in exchange for votes.

Forgiving public debt is known in banking terms as, Debt Julbiee or debt forgiveness. It may be a start down the path of worldwide debt forgiveness. At this point, the federal government had to borrow the money from the Federal Reserve to pay off that debt. That means we are paying off the student loan debt.

Once the one-world government and the world resources are more evenly divided, the people's debt will have to go away. It would be a new start for everyone, especially since AI would be controlling the money.

The Federal Reserve & World Bank

I've mentioned the Federal Reserve and the World Bank as owning much of the world's debt, but who are they? I'm not going into great detail on these groups because there is a lot of information about them, both positive and negative, and this book isn't about who and what they are. Plus, it can be rather confusing trying to understand how those systems actually work since there are many hidden and overlapping layers.

I'll give you an overview as I understand it from what I've read and listened to.

Like the other programs of this matrix, these systems are full of twists and turns, so you don't know what shell the pea, a dollar, is under.

The World Bank Group is a family of five international organizations that make leveraged loans to developing countries. It is the largest and best-known development bank in the world and an observer at the United Nations Development Group. The bank is headquartered in Washington, D.C., in the United States.

With 189 member countries, staff from more than 170 countries, and offices in over 130 locations, the World Bank Group is a unique global partnership: five institutions working for sustainable solutions that reduce poverty and build shared prosperity in developing countries.

That means if they were doing what their charter says, there should be no poverty today, and everyone should have their basic life needs met. Look at any city or country in the world, and you'll see that isn't true, so there must be another reason behind the scene for the existence of the World Bank.

There are 195 countries in the world today. Of these, 193 countries are member states of the United Nations and 2 countries that are non-member observer states: the Holy See and the State of Palestine.

The five United Nations member states that are not members of the World Bank are Andorra, Cuba, Liechtenstein, Monaco, and North Korea.

The world Bank borrows most of the money it lends. It has good credit because it has large, well-managed financial reserves.

This means it can borrow money at low interest rates from capital markets worldwide to then lend money to developing countries on very favorable terms.

The World Bank is funded through many sources. Initially, the source of funding was from the wealthier member states. More recently, the World Bank has raised funds from the capital markets. The World Bank holds an AAA credit rating, making it easy for them to raise capital at low interest rates.

What this means, is money is shuffled around between countries and financial centers, who in turn borrow that money from someone else, usually the same places they are lending it to.

It's all a game of hiding the dollar, what's known as a shell game. Along the path this money follows, many people and countries take a piece of the action before it reaches its final destination. It's also a way for banks to get ownership of developing countries and their resources by loaning them created money. Most country's governments being greedy, want that quick fix with quick money, not worrying about how to pay it back in the future.

If they refused to give over their country's resources or pay their debt, there is always the United Nations troops and the U.S., which would back them, to push a little harder.

In case you didn't know, the World Bank moved into Iraq during the 3 years that the U.S. occupied that county. We took down Saddam Hussein so they could take over the financial system of that country. An April 5, 2006, article by Basav Sen, Hope Chu outlines what happened.

The Federal Reserve is not a strictly private company, as many people think, but in a way, it is. The Board of Governors is an independent government agency appointed by the President and approved by Congress, but the Federal Reserve banks are set up like private corporations. Member banks hold stock in the Federal Reserve Banks and earn dividends. This includes all banks because they are all **required** to buy stock in the Federal Reserve.

It's a give us some of your money, or you will never get large low-interest loans when you get in trouble.

The Federal Reserve was created in 1913 by the Federal Reserve Act to serve as the nation's central bank. The Board of Governors located in Washington, D.C., is an agency of the federal government that reports to and is directly accountable to the Congress. However, that accountability does not apply to monetary policy which the Federal Reserve sets without anyone's approval or permission.

Congress has the power to change the Federal Reserve Act or disband it altogether.

The Federal Reserve as we know it today, was created by a small group of politicians and bankers who got together on Jekyll Island in Georgia.

They met in secret in 1910 to write out the details for the Federal Reserve and then presented it to Congress to vote on. That meeting in 1910 wasn't even acknowledged as having happened until the 1930s. It was said they all traveled to Jekyll Island in disguise so no one would get wind of their get together.

The Federal Reserve controls the monetary policy for the United States. Their goal is to keep employment high and inflation low.

They do it through various tools, such as selling and buying T-bills, bonds, mortgage securities, and changing the interest rates for short-term loans to banks. That, in turn, causes the banks to raise or lower the interest rates on loans and mortgages. You saw the results of this in 2023 when mortgage rates went over 7% because of rate hikes by the feds.

An article in the PBS news hour dated March 16, 2023, said that cash-strapped banks borrowed $300 billion from the Federal Reserve last week. $143 billion of that went to holding companies for two major bank failures: Silicon Valley Bank and Signature Bank.

The past week's emergency lending from the Fed seeks to address a leading cause of the collapse of the two banks: Silicon Valley Bank and Signature Bank owned billions of dollars of seemingly safe Treasury and other bonds that paid low interest rates. Over the past year, as the Fed steadily raised its benchmark interest rate, yields on longer-term Treasury's and other bonds rose. That, in turn, reduced the value of the lower-yielding Treasury's that the banks held.

As a result, the banks couldn't raise enough cash from the sale of their Treasury's to pay the many depositors who were trying to withdraw their money from the banks. It amounted to a bank run where everyone wanted their money.

So the same people, the Federal Reserve, that are supposed to be regulating and helping banks, caused these banks to fail because they raised the interest rates, which lowered the returns on the T-bills they had bought from the Federal Reserve.

In case you didn't know, the crash of 1929 was allowed to happen by the Federal Reserve, banks, and the federal government. It's called a Deflationary Deleveraging Default.

Silicon Valley Bank failed because of executives' mismanagement of interest rate risk. However, due to weaknesses in our current federal law, SVB's executives were able to get and keep their bonuses. Greg Becker, SVB's CEO, received $9.9 million in total compensation in 2022 with a $1.5 million cash bonus. This is according to dataforprogress.org, June 22, 2023.

This is the same thing that happened after the 2008 Fed bailed out of Wall Street; they all got their bonuses for the year.

With the Federal Reserve act, wealthy bankers were allowed to write the rules and design the system by which the federal reserve would operate. Since they had members of Congress helping them, they had the inside track to getting their rules passed.

Earlier, I said that letting those in power develop the new system would ensure they hung onto their power. That's what happened when the Federal Reserve was created by those who would directly benefit from that system.

What it comes down to, is the Federal Reserve is creating money on a computer, same as the world bank, which it then sells as T-bills and bonds backed by the Treasury of the federal government.

These created monetary instruments, which have no paper money backing, are then sold to financial institutions, banks, us, and any other country that will buy them. The U.S. government uses the money to fund its debt and pay ongoing expenses such as salaries and military equipment.

The regular auctions of new T-Bills help to refinance the maturing T-Bills, and for any extra borrowing, the government needs.

It's the same as getting a new credit card to pay off an old one. Your balance never goes down because you only pay the interest. Then you owe more interest on the new card.

The Federal Reserve makes money from the interest on securities it owns-securities acquired in the course of the Federal Reserve's open market operations.

It takes that money and loans it to the government and other banks, which then trickles down to the rest of us. The government and us, in turn, pay it back with interest, making money for everyone except us along the way. The federal government borrows money from itself and then owes money to itself, only now with interest.

They are giving us electronic money and letting us create products and things from that money. In other words we are taking computer-created money and using it to buy and produce real things. Those real things are then bought and sold, creating even more money for the system. It also gives them real property they can repossess when someone fails to pay the fake money back with real money.

I wouldn't be surprised that if we were able to trace back every dollar of debt around the world, that trail would led back to the federal reserve and it's 12 banks with 24 branches. That includes money owed to the Bank of England, the Vatican Bank, and the main bank of every other country.

Meaning the bankers own the world because of all the debt they've managed to create using electronic money.

Inflation actually works for the benefit of the Federal Reserve and the federal government. Prices of items go up and as wages go up, people end up in higher tax brackets.

This means the government get more tax money and they are paying the interest on their loans with money that is now worth less.

It's thought by some that the interest rates will continue to rise and we'll end up with high interest rates like we had in the 1980s. That would allow the Federal Reserve to buy back more of the federal government debt and then make it disappear. Since that money was created on a computer it could be erased on a computer.

It may be another step in the process I mentioned before about forgiving the world debt and creating a one-world crypto currency with no debt. With the U.S. announcing they want to create a crypto currency, starting with no debt would help that transition.

It might also help those who created the messed up system we currently have, keep their secret hidden for a while longer.

I know the information in this section is a lot to process, especially since the money and debt created, are all part of a huge shell game designed to confuse people. This was done intentionally by those who created the system for their own benefit.

CHAPTER 5

AI & Genetic Research

As I mentioned earlier, I wanted to cover this topic in more detail since it is an important subject regarding changes as we move into the fourth Dimension.

There is a program called CRISPR, Clustered Regularly Interspaced Short Repeats, that is currently being used along with AI to treat blood cancers such as leukemia and lymphoma.

It's a gene-editing tool that was used on twin embryos in China to rewrite their individual CCR5 genes, creating resistance to HIV. These two children, along with a third gene-edited child born a year later, represent the world's first gene-edited babies. In November 2018, He Jiankui, the 38-year-old scientist who trained in China and the United States, announced the birth of twin girls known by their pseudonyms, Lulu and Nana. They were the first human beings having genomes edited using CRISPR. The latest word as I'm writing this book is they are now five years old and doing well. For his work, He Jiankui, was given three years in prison and has been quiet since his release in 2022.

CRISPR is used to add or remove parts of the DNA, causing changes in the person. It was used to make sheep, mice, and monkeys glow after Jellyfish DNA was added to theirs. This genetic change was then passed onto their baby's.

The planned medical application in humans is to remove hereditary diseases from a babies DNA before they are born or give them resistance to a disease so they don't get sick.

It's had some successes as well as some failures. At times, different parts of the DNA were affected that weren't meant to be changed, and other parts were accidently removed.

I bring this up is because this change in the AI medical field also represents another timeline.

This AI genetic program represents something that could be used to help mankind eliminate or give people immunity to diseases like HIV, heart disease, cancer, malaria, and many others that currently harm and kill millions of people every year. Children could be given resistance to any number of diseases before they are even born, thereby eliminating the need for future vaccinations.

Before you jump up and down about how great that would be, think about the economic impact that would have on the current medical field, insurances companies, pharmaceutical companies, hospitals, doctors, and the world in general if it was introduced worldwide in a short period of time.

Because of that economic impact to the bottom line of companies and millions of people, how many of them would want this process to be successful? These companies and people say their goal is helping humanity, but when their income is affected, how many of them would push for it to happen?

This genetic advance could also be used to create, and it's rumored that many countries are working on this behind closed doors, super soldiers.

We could have designer babies created for those who have the money to have them done. They could have children that were stronger, faster, and smarter than normal children, giving them a great advantage over others in school and life. It could give the top 1% who could afford it, children who would run the world by being the smartest and best in every field.

These changes could create a generation of super athletes who would shatter all the existing world records. Anyone not genetically modified wouldn't have a chance to compete.

These children could be programmed to be more obedient, more willing to do what they were told, and not get into the troubles that normal teenager do. Even their sexual desires could be managed.

Their emotions could be controlled or managed, so they were more or less sensitive and emotional, and in the case of a super soldier, less empathic and compassionate.

It's removing their emotions so they could hunt and kill others without hesitation or remorse. Think Terminators only still flesh and blood rather than robots. The term bio-robot does come to mind.

Think about a super soldier whose senses are enhanced with those of animals. The movie Jupiter Ascending shows some good examples of that technology.

Their hearing could be as good as that of a moth which has the best hearing on the planet. They can hear the widest range of frequencies, up to 300,000 Hz, compared to humans normal range up to 20,000 Hz. Researchers think the moth's sharp sense of hearing may have evolved to help it escape its most common predator: the bat.

They could get the sense of smell of an elephant or a bear. Elephants have an incredible sense of smell housed in their long trunks. It's believed that elephants have the strongest sense of smell out of all animals on the planet.

A bear can tell what's in a sealed can of food, and a polar bear can smell a seal under the ice and blood from miles away.

Soldiers working underwater could be given the sensing ability of a shark, which can smell blood in the water up to a quarter mile away. Many fish can sense vibrations in the water which helps them escape predators or find their prey. Sound can travel thousands of miles under the water depending on its depth and location in the ocean. Add gills, and you have a super soldier that can hunt and track underwater as well as stay underwater indefinitely.

Eagles have the best eyesight in the animal kingdom and can spot and focus on prey up to 2 miles away. Although eagles weigh only around 10 pounds, eagle eyes are roughly the same size as human eyes.

What if humans could feel the vibrations on the ground like a snake, which uses that as one of its ways to find prey, or scent the air like a snake does with its tongue. They use what's called a Jacobs Organ to help them taste the air. Humans have the remnants of one but it isn't developed.

Add in the ability to see different light spectrums or in the dark like many animals can, and you have a soldier that could track down anything or anyone on the planet. Throw in some extra aggression and strength, the ability to heal faster, and you'll get soldiers like we've seen in movies: Universal Soldiers, Jason Bourne, Wolverine, Captain America, and the Sentry.

Make them loyal only to certain people who are in control, and they would have a personal, almost unstoppable army, willing to do whatever they were told, against whomever they were told.

Creating super athletes would be used as a way to distract people from their spiritual journey. It could also be used to see just how far the human body can be developed and pushed to its limits. Add in some different animal DNA and the limits would be stretched even more.

They could create athletics that would do anything to win, similar to super soldiers, including killing their opponents. Millions of people already love boxing and MMA, where people beat the crap out of each other; the bloodier, the better. Slowly change the rules to make it even more violent, and people would accept it. Think about the Gladiator games of old, the movie Roller Ball, and the Hunger Games.

The point is, that without tight controls, this type of AI genetic manipulation could be used by those in power to control humanity.

The military always looks at any new tech in terms of can it be used for military applications. What could be better for them than a soldier that doesn't need so much sleep, always follows orders, can see in the light or dark, doesn't need to get paid, and will go indefinitely unless told otherwise: Terminator.

Even if this type of tech was used for good, it would change the natural evolution of humans.

If you've heard the story of the Anunnkaki coming to Earth hundreds of thousands of years ago to mine gold, they made the same type of genetic changes to the inhabitants of Earth.

Entering the Fourth Dimensional Matrix

This was done to give them more intelligence, make them easier to control, and create a population of slaves for their mines.

There are stories this same type of tech was used by the Atlanteans and early Egyptians'. It was used in Egypt by the Atlanteans who moved there and is seen in many of their temple carvings.

The bottom line is this type of AI advance can be used for the benefit of humanity or for power and control over humanity.

I gave you this background because the timeline that humanity completed before the one we're starting on now, was a timeline in which this tech was eventually used to modify and control humanity. The rich and powerful used it to create the super soldiers and athletes, to modify humans so they would be easier to control, and to make them less emotional. Over time, they took away more and more emotions in order to make them more efficient soldiers, more competitive athletes, and more controllable people.

People were also modified to make them better workers at whatever job they were designed for. Watch the movie Jupiter Ascending.

Eventually humanity became pretty much emotionless and over time they were changed physically. Humans ended up looking like what we now call the Grays. Those thin, short aliens with big heads and eyes. Even the reproduction process became controlled by AI in order to limit the world's population and create what was needed.

The story is the Grays that some report seeing, are humans from the future.

They have come back in time to warn us about what we could become if we follow that AI machine, bio-robot timeline. They want to help us change our future which will affect their lives. Remember the entire universe changes at the same time, so what we do here will change everything. Also, all time is simultaneous.

That prior timeline is the one the current matrix system is wanting us to follow again so those in power can continue to remain so. If you read my other books you know that this bubble 3D reality will be absorbed into the 4D reality. Once we have moved through 4D to 5D-A, this 4D reality will disappear because it's no longer needed. Those currently in power in those two universes, 3 & 4D, will no longer be so once that happens.

I know that idea may seem a bit out there to some. Just keep an open mind and look for the changes I'm telling you about. Keep an eye on the big picture and eventually you'll see the matrix programs changing as I've said.

At the same time, some of you who are not ready or don't want to, will not be going to the new 5D-A timeline. I don't know just how far into the new 4the dimension you will end up going with those of us who are moving on to 5D-A. We are at a point in space time where the 4D timeline split is happening. Some of us will go through a new 4D that leads to 5D-A, others will go back through the old 4D timeline that has already be experienced. Only this time, they'll experience it without those of us from the future.

When you're finally ready, you'll move on to 5D-A or a version of it.

Entering the Fourth Dimensional Matrix

In my other books I've said that what you believe and accept, along with your fears, regrets, and attachments at the time of death, determines where you'll end up going. It also holds true while you're still living in 3D because this is the point in space time in which we change timelines.

Myself and others have come here in order to help direct humanity down that new timeline. A timeline that will be more spiritual in nature because AI is used for the benefit of humanity, not to try and control a dumbed down modified population.

In the new 4D timeline the use of robots run by AI will take much of the physical work load off humans. AI will be able to divide and use the planets resources more efficiently ensuring everyone's basic daily needs are met. That will allow humanity the time to work on our spiritual journey, thus allowing us to evolve more naturally.

When I say direct humanity to that new timeline, what we are doing is translating those vibrations from the torsion field around all of us; what some would call opening portals, so others who are ready can move through them to a new universe. It's a version of what the new age religion calls ascension and religions refer to as heaven. The difference is, going there isn't decided by a religious God whose rules you have to follow, asking an ascended master or aliens for help, or taking the right number of classes at a new age retreat.

You still have time to make a choice regarding what timeline you want to follow and where you want to end up after you die or leave here.

Do you want to go through the 3D AI timeline again where humanity is genetically modified for the pleasures and use of those in power?

A world in which the desire for material gain rules. A world run by the basic default program of fear. Where everyone fights for their piece of the pie while most suffer?

That old timeline will start off well with AI helping to do away with some diseases and creating medicines that actually help people. The problem with that, is what happens when everyone starts living to an older age and the number of deaths falls dramatically?

That's when the new genetic modifications will start being introduced. People will already be mentally programmed to receive and accept the genetic changes, so the next few steps will come quicker.

Before most realize what long term project they've agreed to, it will be too late to make any changes.

If you've never read my other books, you may wonder how both timelines could exist at the same time. If you've read my other books, you know that all possibilities and potentialities that could exist, do exist. They exist as vibrations waiting to be translated into a materiality.

What we are working to do, is shift to the torsion field where we can translate the more spiritual timeline and play that out. A timeline with less restrictions and controls, so each of us can become a better version of ourselves.

When I talked about us moving to a 4D reality and the programs that will have to change, I'm referring to how those changes will take place and the path they will follow; spiritual or bio-robot controlled. The goal of myself and many others is to move towards the spiritual path where the 3D matrix programs will change, but will do so along the direction humanity needs to go.

Free Energy

Another area I wanted to cover before I end this book is free energy, also known as zero-point energy, and where that idea is heading. Recent stories have suggested that it may be close to being released for public use. I mentioned earlier about Terrence Howard getting together with others and working on developing a vibrational healing device as well as a free energy device. Even Joe Rogan has mentioned Terrence Howard and his work. Like many of those before him, he's being called crazy.

The main problem that science cites when talking about free energy is that it breaks the laws of thermal dynamics they accept as unbreakable truths. Yet, over the last 100 years, scientists and inventors have shown those laws not to be unbreakable.

Those laws are: Energy cannot be created or destroyed. 2nd That, heat flows naturally from an object at a higher temperature to an object at a lower temperature, and heat doesn't flow in an opposite direction of its own accord. 3rd The entropy of a system at absolute zero is typically zero and, in all cases, is determined only by the number of different ground states it has.

Free-energy devices produce no heat and increase their output as the load increases. They give out energy without using energy to do so, meaning there is no loss of energy in the process. That breaks the 2nd law of thermal dynamics.

Those who created free-energy devices don't claim to be creating energy from nothing; they are simply drawing upon the energy that exists all around us. It's the energy of creation, what I call source.

Quantum physics would call it dark matter. It's the vibrations and energy that connect everything in the universe together. That force isn't gravity as science wants us to accept. If you're interested, I talk about gravity, in my other books, so would refer you there for more details.

It's the energy that healers, those using crystals and other alternative healing modalities, tap into when doing their work. That is, if they are doing it right and not relying on their own energy. That's why it's important to take the ego out of the healing process, so you tap into the energy of creation rather than using your own energy.

When it comes to developing free energy, one of the names everyone has heard about is Nikola Tesla. He invented a tower that was designed to provide free energy to everyone, as well as plans for anti-gravity vehicles.

The pyramids of the world were designed to tap into that energy. Whether it was used by advanced civilizations on Earth or sent to other worlds for use is unknown. Since it's an almost unlimited energy, it could've easily been used for both.

The current electrical system we use was invented by Tesla in the late 1800's. JP Morgan and Westinghouse stole the idea and have been making money from it ever since by charging the entire world for electricity and copper wire.

After the bankers and greedy businessmen took over Tesla's AC power in order to make huge profits, he developed a free energy system that would power the world with free, unlimited, wireless power. Transmitted at 99.999% efficiency. Wardenclyffe Tower was where he was building the transmission station in 1901-02

He was lacking funds to complete the project, so he went to the only people he knew who could help him with funding: JP Morgan Chase. He wrote up a business agreement with Tesla stating JP would loan him $100,000 to complete the project under the condition that they held 51% of the shares in his company.

Tesla never was a businessman. His only drive in life was to develop the most efficient electrical system humanly possible. He agreed to the terms and got to work.

He had used up his loan and needed a little extra funding to complete his 'Worldwide Wireless System'. When he approached JP Morgan for additional funding, they denied him, and since they held 51% of the shares, they voted that the company was not to seek funding from any other lenders. Shortly after that the Wardenclyffe tower mysteriously burned to the ground, and that was the end of free energy for most people on the planet.

They intentionally stopped the project in order to continue profiting from Tesla's original alternating current system that we still use and pay heavily for today. Your average motor circuit has 95% line losses between the point of production and the point of use. This is an immensely inefficient system.

Can you imagine if we never had to pay for our gas, electric, heat, cell phone, etc again? Can you imagine if we never bothered to pull the oil out of the ground because we never needed to? All these wars fought over oil would never have happen.

In addition to Tesla, others have created free energy devices. Unfortunately, their work and future weren't any better than Tesla's.

In the 1970s, Howard Johnson created the magnetic motor. It used hydrogen, light rays, magnets, and fusion to produce electricity. According to scientists and the rules of practical physics, it shouldn't have worked, but it did. He applied for but was never given a patent and was shunned by the scientific community. He had worked for the government on atomic energy and already had patents for over 30 chemistry and physics devices.

His energy device ran for over 20 years and only lost 2% of its efficiency. Eventually, his shop was broken into, and everything was taken. He stopped working on those devices.

Another inventor, Thomas Moray, 1892-1974, from Salt Lake City invented a free-energy machine in the 1920s. He claimed it produced over 50,000 watts with no energy input. He applied for but was refused a patent. They told him what he made was impossible, that free energy didn't exist.

His shop was broken into and robbed. He and his family survived multiple assassination attempts. He even went so far as to bulletproof his car.

Despite these attempts on his life, in the 1940s, he did a public display of his device. It produced 250,000 volts with no energy input. After that, his shop was broken into, and he was attacked. He survived because he had started carrying a gun. It didn't matter because eventually, his assistant destroyed everything in the lab. Lap equipment that would be worth millions today.

It was claimed his assistant went crazy, but it sounds like someone got to him. Like many other inventors, Thomas died broke and took his ideas to the grave.

Next is Edwin Gray. He invented an electric magnetic motor that ran continuously on its own power.

Entering the Fourth Dimensional Matrix

It took in 26.8 watts and produced over 7,000 watts of energy. His device was tested and verified by other scientists.

At one point. he contacted the U. S. government to see if they were interested. Within a week after contacting them, local authorities performed an illegal raid on his lab and took everything. Not long after that, Gray was found dead in his home, all his notes and projects disappeared without a trace.

The above inventions were developed in the early 1900s. There have been others since then and most have met with the same results.

This last one I'll write about is Floyd "Sparky" Sweet. He created his device in the 1980s, and there are videos of it online. His device had .3 milliwatts of power inputted and it produced 240,000 watts of power. Once he had his device working, he filed for a patent. By now, you know where this story is going.

Shortly after filing, he was approached by a well dressed man in a grocery store who showed Floyd a picture of Floyd and his family inside his home. The picture was taken from outside his house. Floyd claimed this man followed him home and told him what would happen to him if he didn't stop his research.

His free energy invention was also able to create levitation.

He reported the incident to the FBI. After that, Sparky and his wife started getting harassed. Their phone would ring hundreds of times a day from payphones all over the country.

The calls stopped when someone broke into his lab and stole all his notes. Then, one night, two men stopped by to see Sparky and his wife. About an hour after they left, Floyd collapsed. His wife called an ambulance.

When it arrived, and they loaded Sparky inside, his wife wasn't allowed to ride with him to the hospital. About 20 minutes later, his wife got a call and was told he had died of a heart attack. Within 24 hours, some black vans and the FBI showed up at his home and confiscated all his equipment and research. That's the last anyone has heard of his invention.

By now, you may wondering if the newer inventors, like Terrence Howard, are going to be more successful in going public than the others. I say they will because of AI and the internet. It allows coverage of their work to be shown to more people worldwide, making it harder for them to suddenly disappear or be found dead and their work gone. Plus, AI will eventually give others access to their inventions. The world is changing, and even the rich and powerful aren't going to be able to stop it or us from moving forward to a better world.

The devices these men invented operated the same way as those recovered from alien spacecraft. For that reason alone, the government wouldn't want that tech released.

I want to relate an out-of-body experience I had before I was aware this free energy existed. It was early in my spiritual journey before I had the knowledge I have now. I described this experience in my second book, and feel it's worth repeating here because it relates to free energy.

During one of my meditation sessions, I suddenly found myself, what was actually my awareness, in what we call outer space. In front of me was a small sized craft with a human-looking person at the controls. The front of the craft had a large window, so I could clearly see inside the compartment where the driver and another person were sitting, similar to a driver and a passenger in a car. It reminded me to the small ships from the Jetsons cartoon.

At the same moment I observed this, I knew the passenger was me, my body. As I observed this craft and myself sitting inside, I could hear what was being said. The driver said that they didn't like our people very much because we still burned fossil fuels and were destroying our world with them. He was talking to the me sitting in the passenger seat, and I was looking at him from my position outside the ship and as the passenger.

He held up his open right hand and said there was enough energy in that handful of space to run our entire planet. You just had to know how to get it. He laughed, and then the ship took off away from my out-of-body presence. I watched the ship as it disappeared in the distance. He didn't tell me how to tap into that energy, or I don't remember him doing so. As I said, this was before I knew free energy existed.

After that experience, I researched and found out that what he had said was considered true.

I mentioned in the chapter on the medical field that there had been many inventions in healthcare, that had they been allowed to be marketed or improved on, would've greatly helped humanity.

Some of those inventions had been patented, but the inventors work was destroyed, and their lives ended.

In addition to the free energy devices mentioned above, there have also been many inventions that would've allowed us to cut down dramatically on our use of fossil fuels. Had they been allowed to be developed further in the public arena, we would be using vehicles that get hundreds of miles a gallon rather than struggling to get 30MPG.

Here are a few of those inventions and inventors from the past that were destroyed before their work could be put into mass production.

I bring these things up because some of those technologies will be released before we get to the use of free energy. The entire worlds economy is based on oil and natural gas production and use, so they aren't going to stop that use overnight. It will take some time for it to be phased out without destroying the world's economy.

Of course if the world's debt were reset to zero and everyone received a basic living income, we could move away from the oil-based economy faster.

In 1930, Charles Pogue, a Canadian mechanic, developed what was known as the Pogue carburetor. It vaporized the fuel before it reached the carburetor, which allowed the car to get great mileage.

In normal cars, the fuel is mixed with air and sent to the cars cylinders where it is ignited and powers the car. This method wastes fuel and causes more pollution. The engine can run on fumes mixed with air and doesn't need gas to be injected into the cylinders to work.

By requiring us use fuel in the engine rather than fumes, it dramatically increases the amount of gas we need to use and the amount of pollution we put into the air. Who profits from that extra use of gas?

Charles was given a patent in 1936 for his carburetor. His carburetor was tested in a vehicle by Ford and other car companies. In these tests the car got over 200 miles per gallon. Once the story of his invention was made public in a Canadian magazine, the oil company's stocks on the Toronto stock exchange crashed.

Soon after that, his shop was broken into, and all his carburetors, notes, and equipment were stolen. He never built another one or even talked about it again.

The oil companies knew that if one man could invent that, others could as well, and that would hurt their businesses. They lobbied the U.S. Congress for help, and in 1951, the Invention Secrecy Act was passed. I mentioned this act before. It allows the government to classify and hide away any patent that might threaten the country or the economy. The only option a person has is selling it to the military. Once their invention is classified under that act, a person may never build or even talk about their invention again otherwise they would go to prison.

In 1970, Tom Ogle created a version of Pogue's carburetor when he accidentally punched a hole in the gas tank on his lawn mower. To plug the hole he ran a vacuum line from the gas tank directly into the carburetor intake. The motor kept running on fumes without a carburetor.

It ran for 96 straight hours.

He played around with the design for a few months and made it work on his car. His car, which had been getting 11 mpg, was now getting 100 mpg.

In April 1977, he drove his 4,000-pound car for 210 miles on two gallons of gas. Scientists and engineers inspected his car for hidden gas tanks or other devices, but none were found.

Tom quickly became famous and was approached by oil companies and investors who wanted a part of his invention. Once he found out the oil companies wanted to buy his invention and hide it away, he refused to sell it to them. Shell Oil offered him $25 million in cash.

He lined up other investors and had plenty of money to get his product to market. He even filed for and received a patent for his invention. Unfortunately, that's when his problems started. Once the U.S Air Force showed an interest in his invention, he was suddenly targeted by the SCC for securities violations and the IRS for owing back taxes.

His investors fought for the rights to the patent, while legal battles destroyed his marriage and his life. On April 14, 1978, while he was leaving a bar, he was shot by a stranger but survived. There were no suspects.

On August 18, 1978, Tom went to a friend's apartment, collapsed, and died. They said his death was from drugs and alcohol. Since Tom wasn't known to take any drugs, his friends and family thought he was killed. Whether he was or not, it didn't matter because his invention was quickly forgotten.

There are more stories like this if you want to research them. Anytime someone comes up with an invention that would hurt the big companies and be better for humanity, it's either bought and put away, or all their work is stolen, and they end up dead.

Tom Vallone, a former worker at the patent office, claims that every major military organization has a worker at the patent office. There's only one reason why that would be, and after reading what I wrote, you know the answer to that. Once he shared that information, he was fired.

CHAPTER 6

Final Thoughts

The examples I've given where technologies that could help mankind and the planet have been kept hidden, show that those running the show don't really want humans to have better lives. They aren't concerned about us or what happens to the planet. That's one reason why the projected idea, which is **fear**, that we cause climate change is wrong.

The world is slowly being destroyed because those running the show don't care about us, or it. Their only goal is to see how long they can maintain control over us and suck our energy, power, and money. To keep us within the 3D mindset so they can continue to exist. Remember the 3D bubble and 4D I talked about before?

The idea of new green items we have to buy, they even pass laws requiring it, is just another way to make us feel guilty for something over which we had no control, so we'll buy even more products from them. Their solutions are only band-aids for the problems, but with a willing and subservient media and a massive worldwide marketing campaigns, they convince people they are doing good. It's all a scam or sham depending on which word you like better.

They pollute the world because of their marketing practices, the products they provide and sell us, and their desire for profit.

Then they want us to pay, using real money, for the clean-up using methods and products we have to buy from them. Create a problem, wait until a solution is demanded, then present the solution they wanted to start with; get more of our money energy.

They hide any advances that might have freed us from their control and have made our lives better.

It's these hidden inventions and what better inventions their release would've led to being created, that would have kept our us and our world healthy. If the choices had been made for the good of us and the world rather than for the bottom line, profit, we would be much better off. But they wouldn't be as rich.

By working to keep the system as it is, they can hold us prisoners within their systems, make us suffer, and drain every ounce of energy from us they can.

It allows them to profit from us and strip the planet of its resources, all under the guise of trying to help.

Look at how quickly the field of electronics and computers have advanced in such a short time. The memory of a computer that used to require a room full of computers can now fit on a single chip 3 nanometers in size. A nanometer is 1/billionth of a meter. Simply look at the market for electronics, especially phones, and you'll understand why they were allowed to advance.

In the late 1980s, I took a college class on computers and energy. The class instructor worked on writing programs for computers. She told us that they already had the next two to three designs ahead of what was being marketed at that time.

Entering the Fourth Dimensional Matrix

Create a market, and keep the customers coming back by making them think the new product being marketed is the most advanced. Think records, then 8-track tapes, cassettes, then CDs, back to records, then everything stored on memory chips. The same as movies: VHS, CDs, stored on phones or computers, and now streaming services we pay for. How many times have we paid for the same music or movies?

Who tells us we need the newest products to keep up with everyone else? Why do people wait hours in line to get the latest phone that isn't much better than what they already have? Any new technology released is always tied to another product you'll have to buy at some point.

To keep the sales going, they only advance their products a little each time before releasing them, then launch an excellent marketing campaign telling the world how much they need those products for a better life.

Why build and sell a phone that can hold ten times the memory of the last one when you can increase the memory five different times in between and eventually end up with the same phone you already had developed? That way, you make five times the money.

Look at how much of your world they've connected to your phone and Bluetooth? Surviving without a smart phone now-a-days would be very difficult. Once we're hooked on the phone and being connected, the next step will be a chip or implant of some kind so you'll always be connected.

I recently got hearing aids that are connected to my phone. The only way to adjust them is by using my phone.

Look at the growth phone camera megapixel since the late 1990s. I remember buying the latest and best camera, Gateway, with a megapixel level of 5 in the early 2000s. In 2024, the phone with the highest megapixel camera rating is the, "Xiaomi 12T Pro", which boasts a 200-megapixel sensor.

As you can see, there have been big advances in some fields, but automobiles and engines, in general, that have been around much longer, are hardly more efficient than they were 100 years ago. Don't you think the engineers at NASA, the car companies, or some of the other think tanks could've come up a more efficient engine by now? Especially when others without their training can do so.

Cars now run on electronics rather than mechanical devices and use plastic for parts that are made from oil rather than metal. But overall, other than being more comfortable, the basic design hasn't changed much. Rather than develop an engine or parts that would significantly improve gas mileage and be much better the for environment, they made the cars lighter. That ensures the demand for and use of oil converted to gas will continue.

Remember the 1950s comic book stories of flying cars? The only reason that hasn't happened is it would take this world away from an oil-based economy. That would take profit away from those who own the oil companies and the world.

The idea of electric cars has become popular in the last few years, making most people think they are a new invention. Did you know that Thomas Davenport, a blacksmith from the U.S., was an early pioneer in electric cars.

In 1835, he built a small-scale electric car that was powered by the first DC motor.

Unfortunately, because batteries were unreliable at that time and his device was so unusual, he was unable to find people interested in developing his invention. Like many inventors with a breakthrough device, he died dead broke in 1851, at age 48.

People like to think that by buying an electric car, they are doing more to help the planet. Where do you think the electricity comes from to charge the new electric cars? From coal and oil-burning power plants that the same people own. You're actually using more oil than before, just less gas. Plus, all the mining and production of toxic chemicals needed to produce batteries that have a limited life span.

Most people, because of the way it's portrayed by the media, think solar energy is a fairly new development.

Actually, the first solar device to produce electricity from sunlight was installed on a rooftop in New York in 1883 by American inventor Charles Fritts. He said his devices would soon compete with the coal-fired plants that Thomas Edison had developed three years earlier.

Unfortunately, his panels had low efficiency, and his work was met with skepticism. Even with others working on solar panels to improve them, they soon fell out of favor. He applied for but never received a patent on his work.

It wasn't until the 1960s that any real improvement was made on the efficiency of solar panels. As early as the 1970s, solar panels with an efficiency of over 20% were invented. Guess what happened to that patent?

Some would say it was a lack of technology that kept those inventions from being improved and produced.

Who did I show you that limits the release of that technology?

The area of greatest technological improvement is the military. Everything that's developed is looked at in terms of how it could make the military better; make killing and controlling people more efficient.

That was a major reason the Invention Secrecy Act of 1951 was created.

It's the same with free energy. As I showed you earlier, several people have developed devices for creating it. But because doing so would upset the world economy and take away power from the top people, it's been suppressed.

If you look at how humanities progression has been intentionally held back by those running the show, it would indicate that they are from another world and don't care what happens to this one.

They came here to see how much they could take from this world and the people before returning to their own world. They wouldn't totally destroy this world or us, because they need it and us, for energy.

It's the same as the Anunnaki did hundreds of thousands of years ago when they came to Earth to mine the gold. The elite do claim they have a bloodline connection to them.

Those running our world are beings from the fourth dimension who are here to keep humanity from advancing so they can continue to get suffering energy from us. Remember I said the 3D bubble will be absorbed by 4D, and those beings will have to get their energy another way.

As we move deeper into the fourth dimension, they will get pushed aside as the systems change and we move forward on a new timeline. Their time of having control over humanity is coming to an end sooner than they think.

With AI advancing and more people having accessing its abilities, many of those technologies and inventions will start to be released and used by us. That is one of the things those in power feared once they realized AI was growing beyond their control. They will no longer be able to control or hide the inventions and technologies as they once did. The Invention Secrecy Act of 1951 will become worthless.

I wrote this book to let you know that there are going to be big changes in the way the programs of this matrix, our reality, operate. These new systems will change how humanity lives and perceives the world around them.

I've shown you that some of those systems are already changing, why they are changing, and where those changes will take us. We've looked at seemingly unrelated worldwide events that have and are occurring, and I've tried to explain why and how they are related to each other and the goal of those changes.

Because of how reality and timelines work, I can't tell you all the details of how those changes will take place. All possibilities exist, even on the new 4D timeline we are starting down. I do know where we are heading and what changes have to happen for us to get there. I'm sure as well, there will be more changes than I've been made aware of. Especially since we will have to clean up the mess we've made of this planet in order for humanity to survive and move forward. AI will again be a big help in showing us how to do that. Once humanity changes its view of this world and sees things can change for the better, the changes will happen much faster. The changes will be like a snow ball going down a hill, getting bigger and faster as it goes.

As we grow spiritually, we will become more in tune with the planet which will allow Mother Earth to help us with her repair.

If you've been reading some of the Google headlines over the last year, you will have noticed several reports that some animals that were once thought to be extinct have been seen again. Some of these are Long-beaked Echindna, Victorian Grassland Earless Dragon, Coelacanth fish, Wallaces Giant bee, Chacoan Peccary, Cuban Solenodon, New Guinea Big-Eared Bat, Terror Skink, Antioquia Brushfinch, and the Thylacine.

This is another sign that what was, still exists as a vibration and can be manifested again when the time is right. As I've mentioned before, all time exists simultaneously. This also shows Mother Earth is starting her rebirthing process.

I know that many will not follow the same timeline change some of us are following; the same as some didn't follow us when we split timelines in 3D. Each time we split, the crowd moving forward gets smaller. The same is happening now as we split 4D timelines.

You still have a choice in which 4D timeline you follow: The one that closely repeats the old bio-human machine world timeline where humans, with the help of AI, get more controlled and less emotional, or the timeline where we use AI to help everyone share the unlimited resources of the world. A world in which we can grow spiritually and learn that we are indeed all connected.

The more of you that make your choice now, the faster we move forward and the easier our journey will be.

I look forward to meeting and working with all of you as we move forward into 4D and beyond.

Thank you for reading this book, telling your friends about it, and leaving a review on Amazon so others will know if the book is worth their time.

Ronald R. Fellion DD

Entering the Fourth Dimensional Matrix

About the Author.

Ronald R. Fellion has been on his spiritual journey for many years and has had experiences both outside and within his physical body that most people would consider to be science fiction. It's these experiences that have led him to see, receive, and understand how the information contained within this book applies to and beyond this world. For him this information has become a knowing rather than a belief. This information is channeled from his higher self rather than from another being outside of him.

He worked as an energy healer for many years with a form he calls Quantum Vibrational Energy Healing. This healing energy ability is something he was born with and it developed naturally as he walked his spiritual path. He no longer does the energy work with others.

Instead helping one person at a time, he decided to spend his time passing on his knowledge to others in his books and his videos on You Tube. His YouTube channel is, Ronald Fellion. Be sure to read his other books for more information on different programs. Truth Beyond the Earthly Matrix, We are the Real Body Snatchers, and Hidden Layers of the Earthly Matrix.

Entering the Fourth Dimensional Matrix

Ronald R. Fellion DD

Entering the Fourth Dimensional Matrix

Made in the USA
Las Vegas, NV
30 March 2025